RACE AGAINST TIME

RACE AGAINST TIME

A History of Race Relations in The Lutheran Church-Missouri Synod from the Perspective of the Author's Involvement
1920-1970

ANDREW SCHULZE

Published by
The Lutheran Human Relations Association of America
Valparaiso, Indiana

Printed by North State Press, Inc., Hammond, Indiana

Preface

If there is a single word which summarizes Andy Schulze's life and work, it is the word "Nevertheless." His whole life is a summary of this particular word. He was a great objector and debater. He faced all of life's confusions, frustrations, sufferings and disaster and said to all of it: "Nevertheless." He saw that this word was true in the crucifixon of Christ and all the evidences of evil. It was true of Judas, Caiaphas, Pilate, and the mob.

"Nevertheless." "On the first day of the week as it began to dawn . . . ." This was the total review of his life and a complete resume of it. I discovered that most clearly during the days when he was held in a Southern jail. There he was, with the rats and evidences of forgotten days and lost battles, except for an expression of polite interest on the campus and an evidence of that interest by some money which I had sent him. It was little enough, and yet, there it was again: "Nevertheless."

The word summarized Andy's philosophy of history and its eventual outcome. He knew what the end would be. He had read it in Second Peter 3:10: "The heavens will pass away with a loud noise, and the elements will be dissolved with fire, and the earth and the works that are upon it will be burned up." "Nevertheless." Here was Andy's fundamental faith and confidence. This basic idea led to some strange things in his life. It made him tremendously interested, of course, in the underdog as well as the main possibility of making the minority position a majority situation.

Mr. Chesterton once said: "A saint is one who exaggerates something that the world has forgotten." This was remarkably true of Andy and his attitudes over against the many facets of the race question. He exaggerated something which the world had forgotten. So at times it seemed to us that his unusual emphasis and interest in the problems of the minority — the Blacks — was an exaggeration. Only later on we discovered that it was a normal emphasis under the eternal view of things.

This preface must, of course, end on a personal note. This was Andy's great contribution to my own life and thought — the exaggeration, the singular emphasis on things which the world had forgotten. In this way he made a great and unique contribution to the life and thought of the people around him. For this we shall hold him in everlasting gratitude.

O. P. Kretzmann

Contents

Foreword

The subtitle of this book, "A history of race relations in The Lutheran Church-Missouri Synod from the perspective of the author's involvement," had been decided on before the first work on the manuscript was begun. It says what the book tries to say. Within the pages of the book the phrase "a picture of our past" is found, and the word "our" has as its antecedent The Lutheran Church-Missouri Synod. But this word "our" can be less provincial than the subtitle may suggest. It can very well include Lutherans in this country other than those of The Lutheran Church-Missouri Synod. Indeed, the members of none of the major church bodies are excluded from the laudable things that the book uncovers, nor need they assume that the "dirty linen" of the Missouri Synod which is hung out in the book is greatly different from their own. It is my opinion that every knowledgeable student of the same period of history will find that the story of the Missouri Synod in the main reflects the story of the other major denominations in the area of race relations. If this is the case, the word "our" referred to above may well be interpreted by many others to include themselves, and when they do they too may read the book with interest and profit.

The basis for what I have written is *what I remember,* for I not only lived during the major part of the history under discussion; I was involved in it. In most instances, though, I was able to check and countercheck the accuracy of what I remembered. In this connection, the correspondence which accumulated in my files over a period of more than forty years has proved very helpful.

In August 1968, shortly before I began writing the manuscript, I selected from my files all pertinent correspondence and presented it to the Valparaiso University Library for microfilming. The microfilm is now in the possession of the Library and the correspondence itself has been deposited in the archives of Concordia Historical Institute on the campus of Concordia Seminary in St. Louis. The correspondence as well as the microfilm are at the disposal of anyone who wishes to probe further into the history which the book discusses.

Until the second draft of the manuscript was completed, I had only included the names of those persons involved in the narrative whose

1

words and deeds were, according to my judgment, commendable. I omitted the names of those whose deeds and words I felt compelled to criticize; I thought that was charitable, especially since the great majority of them have already joined the ranks of the "saints made perfect in light." A number of persons who read the manuscript argued that my purpose in writing the book would be better served if the names of all persons referred to would be mentioned. They thought that those reading the book who are acquainted with Missouri Synod history would be led to probe about in their own minds in an effort to decide who was involved and would perhaps on occasion come up with the wrong name; and that would help to distort the historical record. I agreed, and added the names.

Zion on the Mississippi, by Walter O. Forster, was a controversial book setting forth the history of the Saxon fathers of The Lutheran Church-Missouri Synod. I read the book for the first time to see whether the author mentioned the names of such Missouri Synod stalwarts as C. F. W. Walther, Johann Friedrich Buenger, and Ottomar Fuerbringer, even when they made serious mistakes. No doubt for the sake of historical accuracy, *Zion on the Mississippi* gives the names of the "good" men when they were "bad" as well as when they were "good."

The reading of *Zion on the Mississippi* led me to rethink how the biblical writers dealt with this delicate matter. A cursory sampling of the Old and New Testaments revealed that, to save his own neck, Abraham, "the father of believers," gave Sarah his wife over into the hands of the Pharaoh of Egypt; that, contrary to the word of the Lord, Moses *struck* the rock at Meribah; that David, the man after the heart of God, committed adultery and murder; St. Peter "began to invoke a curse on himself and to swear" that he did not know Jesus; because of the seeming incompatibility between Paul and Barnabas, they separated. And, after listing many sins of the Israelites, St. Paul adds, *"they were written down for our instruction."*

Having added the names as above mentioned, I am reminded not only of certain words of the General Confession, but specifically of the way they were once used by our granddaughter, Stephanie, then about two and a half years old. Reluctantly she went to bed for her afternoon nap. Some time later her mother discovered that she was not only wide awake but out of her bed. After several admonitions, she was allowed to come downstairs, and was heard saying, more or less to herself, "I a po', mizzable sinnah." Whether or not I committed the same mistakes made by those whose names were added, I find it necessary to fall on my knees before God and declare myself a "poor, miserable sinner."

I am indebted to a number of persons for taking time to read the manuscript and especially for their helpful criticism. Among them are members of my family, all of whom have had years of personal experience in the church in black communities. Others who read the manuscript and gave helpful suggestions: two former Valparaiso University editors —Professor John Strietelmeier, Consulting Editor, *The Cresset,* and Anne Springsteen, LHRAA staff member, editor, *The Vanguard;* Professor Karl E. Lutze, my successor as executive secretary of the Lutheran Human Relations Association of America; Dr. Clemonce Sabourin, pastor of Mount Zion Lutheran Church in Harlem, and former president of LHRAA; and the Rev. Walter M. Heyne, also a former president of LHRAA.

One more name must be added, that of my wife Margaret, whose dedication to meticulous detail and whose time-consuming assistance in research and typing made the preparation of the manuscript possible. If the book is worth its salt, she should be given the title of co-author.

Chapter One

The Church and Church-related Institutions

Two events transpired in the year of our Lord 1896 which should be recorded in history books for generations still unborn. My mother, if she were still here, would attest to the fact that one of these events must stand out indelibly above the other; and for some years now I have relied on her judgment in such matters. That it really happened, the reader can take my word for it: after more than three score years and ten, I am living proof of this earth-shaking event—I was born.

In later years, when written proof was required, I sought authentic documentation. But the old court house in Cincinnati had burned to the ground, and my birth record as well as other lesser data were irretrievably lost. The family Bible might have noted this important event, but it too seemed to have disappeared. There was but one other source that held promise of proof: the record of my baptism. The church secretary, when asked, sent this information: Andrew Schulze was born on March 8 and baptized on March 22, 1896.

My mother was no student of history. Knowing her as I did, I am quite sure that many politically earth-shaking events might well have taken place without her knowledge and without her being disturbed by them. But if the other event referred to above took place before I was born, I must have reacted to it in such a way as to have made things uncomfortable for her; and if it happened after March 8th, I must have gone into some kind of tantrum the like of which Mother had never witnessed in any of my older siblings. In either case, she must have sensed something had happened to which I, her child, had reacted in such an unusual and, to her, disturbing manner. That other event was the handing down of a pronouncement by the U.S. Supreme Court, known as the Plessy-Ferguson decision, declaring racial segregation constitutional and therefore in keeping with the law of the land.

In all honesty, though, I must confess that I had no conscious knowledge of this "separate but equal" decision, as far as I can remember, up to the very day that, at the age of twenty-three, I arrived in Springfield, Illinois, to study theology in preparation for the ministry.

Holy Trinity—Closer to Heaven

It was a typical early September afternoon when I arrived in the city made famous, not by the seminary that I was to attend, but by the fact that here the great emancipator, Abraham Lincoln, lived, practiced law, and is buried.

The day was warm, and the wind was blowing dust and dry, fallen leaves into the air. I had arrived on a train from Flora, Illinois, one of the few stops of the mainliner running from Cincinnati to St. Louis. The trip to Flora had been somewhat pleasant and comparatively clean, but accommodations on the branch line were less than elegant. The few passengers in the coach in which I rode closed the windows to keep out the smoke and soot of the locomotive only to open them again when the heat became unbearable.

With this experience behind me, I was perhaps not too presentable when I boarded the streetcar heading for the "practical" Springfield seminary. The conductor matter-of-factly told me where to get off the trolley. I had learned through a number of unpleasant experiences when I was in the U.S. Navy during World War I, when on shore leave, always to inquire, at least once, where to get off a train, a bus, or a streetcar.

A Negro gentleman, who no doubt had heard my inquiry, stopped in front of me as he was about to alight, to give me further information about getting to the seminary; and, pointing to a small frame church nearby, he added, "Come and worship with us some time."

That was the beginning. That invitation, no doubt under the providential guidance of the Spirit of God, started me on a path of life on which I have travelled until this day. The next Sunday evening, I went to worship in the little frame church to which Mr. Bates had invited me. On my arrival he was one of the first to greet me.

Life in Springfield at that time had not been profoundly affected as far as housing was concerned by the Plessy-Ferguson "separate but equal" decision. The church was, nevertheless, in a predominantly Negro community. Those who worshipped there, excepting for a few white seminary students and the pastor, were all Negroes.

Edward A. Westcott, a senior seminary student (after graduation, a missionary and later superintendent in the mission field of Alabama's black belt) was already singing in the choir. He and another member of the congregation were the only male members of the choir and they were looking for recruits. I was drafted. To this day I am not sure whether it was the quality of my voice or their urgent need that conferred this honor

5

on me. I nevertheless gladly joined the choir and became its third male member.

There was another congregation in Springfield identified confessionally with the Synodical Conference. Its house of worship was about a mile away. The smaller congregation had no Sunday morning services. Until I became involved in other activities—first in teaching Sunday school and later the Bible class—I could function as a choir member and at the same time follow the Sunday morning trek of the student body, the professors, and their families to the big downtown church.

The big church was known as Trinity and the small congregation *Holy* Trinity. I have often referred to *Holy* Trinity—facetiously, of course—as being closer to heaven than Trinity. Although I do not claim an accolade divine resting upon me, it is possible that the Holy Spirit had His part in the decision-making which caused the bigger and older congregation to be named Trinity and the smaller one Holy Trinity.

In keeping with the spirit of the times, and as far as my knowledge takes me, Holy Trinity was practically a nonentity insofar as the big congregation was concerned. The more I became involved as a student in the work at Holy Trinity, the more I, with Holy Trinity, became isolated from Trinity congregation, its people, and its official district and synodical activities.

The girl who was later to become my wife had been from her baptism until her marriage a member of Trinity Church. (We had first met in another city—a fact which she to this day stresses, I suppose to emphasize that she was not a "seminary-student chaser.") As a child, Margaret, then known as Gretchen, had spent many Sunday afternoons in the Trinity parsonage in the circle of the pastor, Dr. Frederick Brand, and his family. As a young girl and as a teenager she had been active in all the functions of the congregation which her age and sex permitted. But with all this intimate relationship, as Margaret told me later, she didn't know that Holy Trinity Church existed until she met me and began to attend evening services there with me.

In the twenties and until recent times, many pastors of congregations of Negro constituency in the South and the North were white men; and it was not unusual for the pastor's wife to belong to the white congregation in the same town where her husband was the pastor of the so-called Negro congregation. One white pastor in particular, the Rev. Erich H. Wildgrube, Sr., who spent his whole professional life as the minister of a congregation of black membership, said to me, "Show me one passage in the Bible that proves segregation to be sinful!" All during his ministry, I am told, his wife and children attended a white church.

Years later, I was invited to dinner in the home of a white pastor, the

6

Rev. G. M. Kramer, who shepherded a congregation of Negro membership; he was also superintendent of all so-called Negro mission work in his district, and, in matters racial, one of the chief mentors of the Synodical Conference Missionary Board. When I arrived at his home, I found that he was living in a lily-white suburban community miles away from the church of which he was the pastor. I was not in his home very long before his wife began to tell me how disastrous it was for any white family to live in a Negro community. (She probably was unaware of the fact that by this time my family and I had lived in predominantly Negro communities for almost twenty years.) In the presence of her husband and another guest, the Rev. Louis A. Wisler, who was the executive secretary of the Synodical Conference Negro mission work, she said, "If your family lives in a nigger neighborhood, it can only go down and down and down and down."

In Cincinnati, the families of the pastor and the parochial school teacher of a congregation of Negro membership attended a white church. When the pastor accepted a call elsewhere and another pastor replaced him, the new pastor's family attended his all-Negro church and he requested the parochial school teacher to ask his family to do the same. The teacher refused. The new minister's request was supported by another pastor in the same city, the Rev. Walter Littman. When his voice went unheeded by fellow pastors and church officials, he came close to losing his mental equilibrium as well as his congregation.

I had assisted at Holy Trinity during all of my seminary years, and at the time of graduation I was called to be the pastor. Having lived in the state of celibacy as the seminary regulations dictated, I was married soon after graduation and shortly before taking over pastoral responsibilities. It was at this time that my best friend on the seminary faculty, Dr. Theodore Engelder, who was the most liberal in racial matters and had identified himself with Holy Trinity more than any of his colleagues, advised me to have my wife retain her membership at Trinity Church. Margaret never entertained the idea.

The Springfield Seminary in the Twenties

While at the Springfield seminary I had imbibed much of the spirit of the times and did not question the theology which helped to nurture that spirit. Much later in life I realized that the theology of the seminary in the 1920's in the matter of race was reflected in the lives of faculty members and their families and the students generally. When I became conscious of this fact, I understood more fully that the racial attitude of the nation as a whole had been mirrored in the seminary's theology and in those who were influenced by it.

The members of the faculty were not like some theologians of post- and antebellum days—race baiters and negrophobes. If anyone ever asked them in the classroom what they thought about the lynchings taking place at the time, or the revival of the Ku Klux Klan—south and north, even in the neighboring state of Indiana—they probably would have evaded the real issue by responding, "That's a social or political, not a theological problem." If pressed for an opinion on the morality involved, they might well have condemned both lynching and Ku Klux Klanism on the basis of the moral precepts of the Fourth and Fifth Commandments of the Decalogue.

All members of the faculty of that day have gone to their eternal rest and I hold their memory in high esteem as devout men of God who "contended for the faith once delivered to the saints"—as they conceived that faith to be.

Like an active volcano, the race issue was then already smoldering and churning beneath the surface, one day to erupt and to threaten the very life of the church and the nation. As far as I can recall after more than 45 years, the race issue as such was seldom if ever discussed in the classroom. Segregation with all the concomitant ethical problems involved— the generally assumed innate superiority of one race and the inferiority of another, all running counter to the doctrine of creation as taught at the seminary; why no Negroes were enrolled at the seminary during the years that I was there; and the fact that there were two congregations in Springfield, for all practical purposes one for whites and one for blacks —these and many other related questions were not a matter of classroom discussion or debate. Little wonder that many seminarians of those years were ill-equipped to give a responsible theological answer, much less good pastoral guidance to their congregations when both answers and guidance were demanded as racial tension soon thereafter became a matter of national and churchwide concern.

As late as 1965, when I delivered a lecture to a pastoral conference near Chicago—where the racial volcano had already erupted—and spoke of the inadequate theological preparation of our pastors who were at our seminaries in the early decades of this century, a somewhat elderly pastor, a graduate of my alma mater, challenged me. He said the professors often referred to the fact that "we must bring the gospel of Jesus Christ to the colored people." I was glad for the criticism; it emphasized exactly what I was trying to tell the conference.

Talis Rex, Talis Grex

Theological professors, like parents, can very often teach more by

8

example than by precept. This is especially true when theological matters are involved. Lutherans should find no difficulty in accepting this statement. It is not only in keeping with what Luther said; it is a part of their confessional profession. For Luther, in his Small Catechism, in response to the question, "How is the name of God hallowed among us?" answers, "When the Word of God is taught in its truth and purity, and *we as the children of God also lead a holy life according to it.*"

Luther's Catechism is quoted here, not to show that the Word of God teaches that theological professors, their families and their students, in order to "hallow God's Name," must attend Holy Trinity church in Springfield, Illinois, or any other church of similar membership. If, however, the professors thought and taught that racial segregation, especially in the church, was sinful, then one could anticipate that members of the faculty would have demonstrated by their personal example what they taught. The little, segregated, isolated Holy Trinity Church represented a God-given opportunity to put into personal practice what the professors were teaching in the classroom. By and large, though, they, like the big Trinity congregation itself, lived and acted as though Holy Trinity was non-existent.

There were some exceptions. For a number of years Dr. Theodore Engelder acted as assistant to the pastor of Holy Trinity, the Reverend Herbert Claus. From 1917 to 1923 Pastor Claus served two congregations, one in St. Louis, also of predominatly Negro membership. Every second week he commuted to Springfield to serve Holy Trinity congregation. During his absence Dr. Engelder, with the assistance of several seminary students, took charge. When Pastor Claus accepted a call elsewhere, Dr. Engelder became the interim, acting pastor of Holy Trinity.

As far as I can recall, during the eight years that I was identified with the congregation, first as a student and then for four years as pastor, there was an occasional visit to Holy Trinity by several members of the seminary faculty. But they came upon special invitation, chiefly to occupy the pulpit on Sunday evenings.

Almost if not all members of the faculty lived on the seminary campus, in walking distance of Holy Trinity, and closer than Trinity. While Holy Trinity as an institution was in dire need of the type of membership faculty members and their families could have given, none of them became members of Holy Trinity. Perhaps they never thought of it. What is more, although I sensed something to be wrong in the structural organization of Missouri Synod Lutheranism in the town, I never confronted the faculty with the thrilling challenge that one or more of them and their families give consideration to transferring their membership to Holy Trinity. The best that probably can be said for their not volun-

9

tarily doing so, as well as my not suggesting it, was that a theological vacuum existed at the time.

During those years a small handful of seminary students—ten at the most—attended Holy Trinity, while on Sunday morning the big downtown church found its spacious balconies on both sides of the nave filled with seminarians. To this day I am not sure why they sat there. Was it simply a custom that was taken for granted? Was it the result of a congregational resolution? Did they sit there out of personal preference, feeling that they were closer to heaven when they were closer to the preacher way up there in the pulpit? (I am inclined to doubt this, since the sermons were later often subjected to serious scrutiny and carping criticism.) Or was it the carnal nature of the students that gave them opportunity from that vantage point to get an occasional glimpse of the young ladies seated in the nave? As a matter of fact, many seminarians married girls from Trinity; none, however, ever married a girl from Holy Trinity. But that's not the whole story.

Black Girls and White Seminarians

When I first came to the seminary the rumor was afloat that the student leader of the band wanted to marry a girl from Holy Trinity, but was finally dissuaded from doing so. Was it because of a threat that he would not be graduated and thus be refused a call into the ministry? Was it because of anticipated social pressure that would ostracize him from his white family and friends? Or was it because the young lady herself was disinclined to become involved? I do not know.

Every now and then during my years of contact with Holy Trinity congregation, seminary students would confide in me their interest in a certain young lady of the congregation and would then lament the fact that race was a barrier to their following the promptings of Cupid. Later in life, when certain pastors and I had renewed acquaintances, they told me of the same promptings involving the same young lady when they were seminarians. I met with the latest experience of this nature more than forty years after I had moved from Springfield; at the time I was in Germany working on this manuscript.

The young lady in question, Miss Phyllis Jones, was beyond a doubt dark and attractive. But I assumed it was more than that which caused seminarians to be attracted to her. Already in her teens she was an intelligent, refined, and cultured person, much like her parents. But there was much more to recommend her as a prospective Lutheran pastor's wife. She knew why she was a Lutheran, and her whole life interest seemed to be centered in the good news in Jesus Christ and the furtherance of His Kingdom as she had come to understand it. She married a

10

Negro minister of the gospel (not Lutheran) who later took over an important administrative post in a denominational school and still later taught theology at Howard University. Though faithful to her husband in their family and his professional life, she never lost her fidelity to the Lutheran Church in which the Holy Spirit through baptism placed her as a very young child. Was a Lutheran parsonage unworthy of being graced by her presence? And, if so, was the "theological vacuum" at the seminary what kept her out of such a parsonage? (For the author's theology on interracial marriage, see *Fire from the Throne*, St. Louis: Concordia Publishing House, 1968, pp. 129-143.)

We Move to St. Louis—the Citadel of Missouri Synod Lutheranism

The Director of Negro Missions, the Rev. C. F. Drewes, my boss at the time, had suggested as my goal a number of converts per year to the Lutheran Church. But my four years as pastor of Holy Trinity congregation in Springfield, Illinois, were not crowned with success that would make headlines—measuring success by the number of accessions and the amount by which the congregation under my ministry was able to reduce the yearly financial subsidy received from the Synodical Conference. Margaret was my secretary already at that time; and it must have been her faultless typing of monthly reports to the Missionary Board rather than the figures themselves that caused the Board to transfer me to St. Louis. The Missionary Board very likely did not have the slightest idea of the trouble I was to cause them later.

The church to which I was called had been given the typical name "St. Philip's" (see Acts 8:26 ff), typical because of the community in which it had been established and the people whom I was to serve. I came there in the late spring of 1928.

St. Philip's Church was dedicated on May 8, 1927. Margaret and I left our year-old son with her parents and went to St. Louis for the dedication. The afternoon service had just begun when we arrived at the church. The Reverend Marmaduke Nathanael Carter, the well-known black pastor of St. Philip's Church in Chicago, was the guest speaker. An overflowing crowd of worshippers, members of the many white Lutheran churches of the city, together with the charter members and a few brave souls from the community, were in attendance. We found a vacant spot, standing room for two, on the church lawn beside the wife of Dr. Martin S. Sommer, a member of the St. Louis seminary faculty. Mrs. Sommer was at that time president of the St. Louis Ladies Aid for Negro Missions, an organization that contributed substantially toward the cost of the construction of the new church building. Upon invitation of Mrs. Sommer, Margaret shared her umbrella to avoid the hot sun.

11

As I attended the dedicatory service, I had no inkling that within a year I would become the pastor of this church and launch out upon a new ministry which would involve me personally, in a greater degree, in the historical development of race relations in The Lutheran Church-Missouri Synod.

When the church was dedicated, the charter members numbered 17 communicants, almost all of whom lived in a more congested area of St. Louis. Within a year, though, under the pastorate of the Reverend Paul E. Gose, the membership had grown to about one hundred communicants. The great majority of the new members had been members of an African Methodist Episcopal church a block away from the new St. Philip's. Tension had developed in the A.M.E. congregation, causing many of the members to look elsewhere for church connections. KFUO, a local radio broadcasting station identified with The Lutheran Church-Missouri Synod, was reaching into the homes of many of the people of the community. Given these two factors, and adding to them another, the dedication of what at the time was a semi-modern, attractive church building, it is understandable that during the first year after the church's dedication its membership should increase some sixfold. Many of the new members from the community were educated, middle-class people.

The pastorate that I took over was, from an institutional viewpoint of members and dollars, a real bonanza. Although "conversions" to Lutheranism and in many instances to Christianity itself took place in the days of my ministry, that is not the whole story. The members themselves, imbued by the Spirit and aglow with the zeal that is often the possession of those who for the first time know what it means to call Christ "the Lord," told others of their newfound faith.

The economic depression of the thirties struck a devastating blow to the black communities of industrial centers of the nation. St. Philip's congregation, however, with perhaps a third of its employable members unemployed, became the first of the Synodical Conference's so-called Negro Missions to become self-supporting. In two successive years in the very heart of the depression 37 adults were baptized or confirmed on Pentecost Sunday. Other classes were also received into membership during the same two years. The largest number of adult accessions in any of the other Lutheran churches of the city during the same years was 19.

It wasn't long before the church building with a seating capacity of approximately 200 (including the nave, balcony, and narthex), with three services each Sunday, became too small to accommodate the worshippers. A larger church edifice might well have been built or the one then in use might have been enlarged, incidentally adding glamor to glamor. I was determined, however, to lead the congregation along another path. I had seen how congregations had grown so large and so unwieldy that the pastor or pastors could hardly know the members of their own flock, much less serve them in any adequate pastoral capacity; and the institutions themselves were always in danger of becoming self-centered and self-serving.

With the cooperation of the congregation and the help of a few staunch friends (there will be opportunity later to single out some of them), we began to steer a different course. Instead of planning for a big congregation with a big church edifice, we looked over the field where the prospects for membership were outside the territory immediately adjacent to St. Philip's Church. In two such communities new congregations, each with a nucleus of members transferred from St. Philip's, were formed and modest church structures erected. These were Holy Sacraments on West Belle Place and St. Michael in Kinloch.

When I left St. Louis to take up other work, St. Philip's congregation, having released fairly large nuclei of members to form new congregations, and having received less than a dozen members by transfer, had about 700 baptized members, about 500 of them communicants; and the congregation, with a church and parsonage in its name, had a debt of less than $10,000.

Dollars and numbers are not to be the chief objective in the life and work of the church; a faithful witness to Christ is. But financial success and increase in numbers which may result from a faithful witness to Christ must be recognized as the blessing of the Holy Spirit, and good.

Symptoms of Missouri Synod Inertia

Much of the officialdom of The Lutheran Church-Missouri Synod was centered in St. Louis: Concordia Seminary; the many offices of the Synod at Concordia Publishing House, 3558 S. Jefferson Ave.; also the office of the executive secretary of Negro Missions of the Synodical Conference. The unusual numerical growth of St. Philip's congregation very likely did not remain unnoticed by professors and synodical officers, executives and administrators. What disturbed me, though, was the fact that the Synod, which was represented by Concordia Seminary and the offices on Jefferson Avenue, was not prepared as a whole to welcome Negro Lutherans into the full fellowship of the church. Civil rights, too, centered in justice and equity, denied black people in general and black Lutherans in particular, were seemingly of little or no concern to the Synod and often even denied as legitimate concerns of the church.

When I stopped to look at the rapid growth of St. Philip's on the one hand and the attitude of the Synod on the other, I realized that I was sitting on a powder keg, and every additional accession was adding to the explosive situation.

At one time during my St. Philip's pastorate I counted 32 members who had college degrees, no mean number for any congregation in the thirties of this century, and doubly true of The Lutheran Church-Missouri Synod of that time. I knew it would not be long before members of the congregation would challenge the race relations status quo in the Synod and become disillusioned as they learned about it. I did not want that on my conscience.

Another phenomenon that was soon to appear on the scene to help challenge the status quo was the movement of members of the congregation to other cities, some of them students attending colleges or universities. Our churches of white constituency by and large were not ready to receive our members who had moved into their midst.

At first I saw this condition obtaining quite generally in the church as a hindrance to mission work. But when I was still in Springfield, the conviction developed in me that a deadly disease had laid hold upon the mother church that could well destroy it. And so my resistance to the status quo in race relations in the Synod shifted quickly in its primary concern from the mission work of the Synod to the Synod itself, its pastors, teachers, officials, institutions, and its hundreds of thousands of members. Little did I realize then that a movement would emerge in the middle sixties called "Black Power" which says to those whites who were interested in changing the status quo in race relations to work for a change among their fellow Caucasians.

My presence in St. Louis as pastor of St. Philip's congregation from 1928 to 1947 gave me ample opportunity to observe at first-hand what race relations were like in The Lutheran Church-Missouri Synod from the perspective of the citadel of the Synod. My presence there in the capacity of the pastor of a congregation of predominantly Negro membership, crowned with dollars-and-numbers success unequalled at that time by any other congregation of similar membership, gave me a responsibility and opportunity to address myself to the issue of race as it confronted the church.

St. Paul's College, Concordia, Missouri

In 1938 when the membership growth of St. Philip's congregation had reached an all-time high and the children of the adult converts were now being prepared for confirmation, there were 42 boys in two classes. Where are they today? What are their professions or occupations? To give an accurate and detailed answer would go beyond our present

14

purpose. But a sampling can nevertheless be given without time-consuming research.

One received his bachelor's degree from Valparaiso University and is now a medical doctor; one is the managing pharmacist at two medical centers; one has a Ph.D. in physical education and is head of a large rehabilitation hospital; another is a professional diplomat, who at the time of this writing was a high-ranking attache of the U.S. Embassy in Madrid; another, a chaplain in the armed services with the rank of major, has been decorated with the Silver and Bronze Stars and, after serving a year on the battlefield in Vietnam, was the only chaplain on a U.S. military post in south Germany; one is a public school principal; another is a full-time adviser to the governor of New York. A number of them have proved themselves to have a deep and abiding interest in the life and work of the church. But in order to pursue our narrative, we must return to the days when these men were boys and preparing for confirmation.

When I look back to those days, I find many causes for chagrin if not repentance. One is the fact that, though the congregation of which I was the pastor was not a member of the synodical body, I was. And since I was a member and my name was on the roll of the clergy of the district, I received a letter one day asking me to look about among the gifted boys of the congregation who would possibly be timber for the ministry. It was a routine mimeographed letter sent by President Albert J. C. Moeller of St. Paul's College, Concordia, Missouri, I suppose, to all clergy on the Western District roster. No doubt I had received letters of similar intent many times before, when I was in Springfield and after I had come to St. Louis.

As far as I can recall, there were three specific reasons why I chose to take up the gauntlet at this time by responding: race had become a live issue in the nation; I had been involved through many activities; and my congregation had the students St. Paul's College was presumably calling for. Was it an example of my own naivete cropping out again or was it the prompting of the Holy Spirit to be "wise as serpents and harmless as doves" that caused me to answer the letter from Concordia, Missouri, as I did? I do not know to this day. Another reason why I too can live day by day only by forgiveness.

I had on previous occasions learned to know something about Concordia, Missouri, its race ideology, its people, and the role that Missouri Synod Lutheranism had played in its life. It was a small town not far from Kansas City, in a section of the state where some 75 years after the Emancipation Proclamation the people themselves couldn't quite make up their minds that the Civil War was over.

Had St. Paul's College at that time moved elsewhere, not only would the girls of the town and surrounding community have had to look to some other place for beaux, but much of the small-town talk would have languished. Had Concordia Creamery—owned and operated by an upstanding member of a large Missouri Synod congregation—moved, the economy of the community might well have collapsed. More importantly, if all Missouri Synod Lutherans had suddenly moved elsewhere, Concordia, Missouri, would just as suddenly have turned into a typical ghost city.

I knew in a general way the segregationist spirit of the area as well as the race relations status quo of the church in general at that time; and I had no reason to believe that the Missouri Synod Lutheranism of Concordia, Missouri, was different from that type of Lutheranism found throughout the nation. There was, however, one personal experience that caused me to believe that Negro students from St. Louis, or any other place this side of Africa itself, would have been less than welcome in the town or at the college.

While attending a Missouri Synod pastoral conference in the town, I had the good fortune of being one of several guests in the home of the owner of the creamery. If I remember correctly, his hospitality left nothing to be desired. I am sure that the creamery butter was excellent. My host accepted my order for a certain number of pounds to be sent to my St. Louis address at regular intervals. To my amazement, when the first pound was unwrapped I found a printed note giving reasons why people as well as industry would do well to consider making Concordia, Missouri, their home: No Negroes were living there! And I had already arranged for some Negro families to receive some of the butter!

For better or for worse, before venturing to send some unsophisticated teenage Negro students to St. Paul's College, I made inquiry as to whether Negro students would be welcome.

Missouri Synod Board of Directors Votes for Segregation

On May 12, 1938, I responded to the mimeographed letter I had received shortly before from President Moeller. I called his attention to the racial make-up of my congregation, the large number of boys in my confirmation classes, and my hope to be able to accept the college's invitation to send gifted lads to the institution to prepare for the holy ministry.

In spite of the great desire on the part of the faculty and the administration of St. Paul's College to increase its enrollment, they hesitated to invite the boys of my St. Louis congregation. Although there was no

16

scriptural mandate and no synodical resolution forbidding the acceptance of students of a certain specific racial strain, both Scripture and synodical laws and bylaws, by their silence on this subject, should have made the acceptance of such students to be taken for granted. But those in authority at the college thought and acted otherwise.

Less than two weeks after I had written President Moeller, I received a reply from Professor Walter R. Roehrs, the secretary of the faculty, to the effect that the Board of Directors of the Synod "in a meeting on May 18th decided against the admission of colored students to other institutions besides those named and maintained specifically for them by Synod." Which means that in such a short time (a) the college had received and considered my request, (b) the Synod's Board of Directors had been asked to make a decision, (c) the Board of Directors met, decided negatively and informed the faculty of St. Paul's College to that effect, and (d) I was informed of the entire procedure.

It seemed to me then, and does today still, that the Board of Directors devoted little time to a subject that was becoming one of the major issues of the 20th century for church and nation. Did they intend to make short shrift of the matter by nipping the bud of racial revolution before it could bloom?

Soon after I had received final word from the faculty, I wrote the secretary of the Synod, Dr. M. F. Kretzmann, who was also the secretary of the Board of Directors of the Synod, asking him to confirm or deny what the secretary of St. Paul's College had written me relative to the Board of Directors' decision. His response was as follows:

The information which has come to you from the secretary of the faculty of St. Paul's College is correct. Colored students are not to be admitted to our colleges or preparatory schools for several reasons, which seem rather obvious to me. The Synodical Conference maintains a college especially for these boys and it seems the logical thing that our colored students should attend this school just as we, as a rule, maintain separate congregations for our colored Christians. This can hardly be called a discrimination against our Negro Christians. You know that there is in certain localities, especially in the South, quite a feeling that the two races should be kept separate, which seems to work out to the mutual benefit of both the white and the colored people. Of course, you have the privilege of bringing your objections before the Board of Directors, if you are so inclined.

On March 29, 1940, after having consulted a goodly number of persons, including Dr. Walter A. Maier and Dr. George v. Schick, I wrote the Board of Directors of the Missouri Synod, asking that their resolution of

17

May, 1938 be rescinded. On April 19 I received a negative response in which the Board presented substantially the same arguments set forth when they wrote me previously in the same matter.

I never tried to ascertain to what extent the Board of Directors made its segregationist policy known, nor to what degree they tried to implement it. Nevertheless, no doubt can be entertained that the Board's decision was not at all out of harmony with the prevailing mood of the Synod at that time.

St. Louis Seminary Confronted with Issue

To the best of my knowledge, only one Negro was enrolled at and attended Concordia Theological Seminary, St. Louis, before the fourth decade of this century; and he was not graduated. When writing President Moeller of St. Paul's College, Concordia, Missouri, on May 12, 1938, I referred to "the offer made by Dean Fritz [Dr. John H. C. Fritz, Dean of Students] to the effect that any Negro student who has the proper qualifications can matriculate at the St. Louis Seminary." It was not long after the dean had made that statement to me that the policy expressed in it was to be challenged; whether the challenge was a result of the segregationist policy adopted by the Board of Directors of the Missouri Synod, I do not know.

Jeff Johnson, a third-generation Lutheran, was enrolled at Concordia College, Oakland, California, in February 1942. In 1944 his name along with others of his classmates was sent to the St. Louis seminary for matriculation. Word somehow got through to the faculty that Jeff was a Negro.

At that time already there were several if not a goodly number of the seminary faculty who, if they had known of the policy adopted by the Board of Directors of Synod, would have opposed it on theological grounds. One of them, Prof. Alfred M. Rehwinkel, told me that Mr. Johnson's enrollment was to be challenged on the basis of his racial background and asked for information with which to bolster his argument in favor of the enrollment of Mr. Johnson. He was enrolled, and was graduated from the seminary in 1948. He shepherded congregations in Detroit, East St. Louis (Illinois), and Indianapolis. After receiving a Ph.D. degree, he became a member of the faculty of Valparaiso University in 1962.

Where to Enroll our Sons

Our three sons, Paul, Herbert, and Raymond, had indicated from time to time their desire to study for the ministry. When Paul was to be graduated from high school in 1943, we were confronted more personally with the challenge thrown down by the Board of Directors of the Synod in 1938.

It was evident that the St. Louis seminary had not abided by the 1938 ruling in the case of Mr. Johnson. Was his enrollment to be considered an exception to the rule since he had already been graduated from Concordia College in Oakland? And, if so, were we to anticipate that any of the ten or more preparatory schools covered by the ruling of 1938 would reject black students wishing to be enrolled, as St. Paul's College in Concordia, Missouri, was prepared to do? We had to know before enrolling our own son in one of them. We could not, for conscience sake as well as for the well-being of our congregation and others of like membership, enroll our son where their youth were not permitted to enroll.

The nearest preparatory school other than St. Paul's at Concordia, Missouri, was Concordia College, Milwaukee, Wisconsin. I wrote President Leroy C. Rincker, describing what had happened in 1938, and concerning our desire to enroll our son in his school, but of our unwillingness to do so if his school would not be willing to enroll our Negro boys. If the Board of Directors of the Synod had taken steps to implement their decision of May 18, 1938, President Rincker knew nothing about it. He wrote to the Board of Directors informing them that, if he received no word to the contrary, he would enroll black students when the opportunity presented itself. (Before final word from the president of Concordia, Milwaukee had been received, I had written to the Wisconsin Synod college in Watertown, Wisconsin, and was informed that they were ready to receive black students.) The president of the Milwaukee school did not receive a negative answer, and so our son Paul was enrolled there. In 1951, our youngest son, Raymond, and soon thereafter Lindsay Robinson, a member of St. Philip's Church in St. Louis, were enrolled at the Milwaukee Concordia.

Springfield Seminary Found Wanting

At the dawn of the 20th century the missionary work of the Synodical Conference was flourishing in Louisiana and in the Carolinas. And what was not the case later in the history of that work, young Negro men, under great handicaps, were volunteering to prepare for the ministry. To do so at the time meant they would have to go north for their education, study at a seminary where German was the medium of instruction, and subject themselves in many ways—including, I suppose, eating sauerkraut several times a week—to a culture quite foreign to them.

Very shortly after the turn of the century, five Negro students were enrolled at the Springfield seminary. Their going there was not only a mark of faith and courage on their part, and evidence of thorough and

19

effective work by the white missionaries who had been their pastors and teachers; it was also a mark of a racially liberal spirit on the part of the seminary authorities of that day, of synodical officials, and perhaps to some degree of the communicant membership of the Synod as well.

This same spirit seems still to have been in evidence in 1908. The seminary at that time (and it does still) bordered on a predominantly black community. When a race riot took place in Springfield in August of that year, the seminary housed and protected scores of Negroes until the riot had been quelled.

[To understand what happened at the seminary in those days, it may be well to remember that the German people who had recently immigrated to the United States were by and large politically liberal; they became members of the Republican Party which at that time and until perhaps 1912 was the liberal party. But with the passing of several decades and when the Democrats became the liberals, those of German background—by that time the third and fourth generation in this country—had become politically conservative and remained with the once liberal but now conservative Republican Party.]

Whether the Springfield seminary had heard of the 1938 decision of the Board of Directors of the Synod, that Negroes were to be directed to the institutions established for them, or, conversely, whether the seminary authorities knew that a Negro had been graduated from the Oakland preparatory school in 1944 and was soon to be graduated from the St. Louis seminary, I cannot say. There is evidence, though, that my alma mater was not going to enroll Negroes at this time.

Between 1946 and 1947 several of us made what proved to be abortive attempts at re-opening the Springfield institution to black students, and thus re-establishing the racially liberal image it had at least until 1908.

Samuel L. Hoard, from his early teens and until his discharge from the U.S. Marines in 1945, seemed to have had but one ambition—to become a Lutheran pastor. (He was the only member of his family who was a Lutheran at that time. What drew him to the Lutheran Church when he was about twelve years old was the contrast he observed between the positive and evangelical tone of the Lutheran sermon and Sunday school lesson and what he later described as the "hell-fire" legalistic message he had been accustomed to hear in his family's church.)

Sam was told of what seemed hopefully to be three possibilities; and he would have to make the choice. (They are not listed here necessarily in the same sequence in which they were expressed at that time, nor in the order of their relative importance.) He was told about Immanuel Lutheran College and Seminary at Greensboro, N.C., of Concordia Seminary in his home town (St. Louis) as well as the preparatory training that would still be required for his matriculation there, and of the so-called practical seminary in Springfield, Illinois.

The institution at Greensboro was for all practical purposes a second-rate, segregated school, operating under the auspices of the Synodical Conference. For Sam the Greensboro college was out of the question. To what extent his objection to attending that institution was based on theological grounds may be hard to establish. Although, and perhaps because, he had experienced the sting of the segregation system in St. Louis and in the armed services, he knew the horror stories that other Negroes who had come from the South had told him. He would have none of it. He wouldn't consider Immanuel College, a thousand miles away in the South.

The St. Louis seminary seemed enticing. It was in his home town; he had seen the place on a number of occasions, and St. Louis seminarians were always, at least during the school year, present and participating actively in many phases of the life and work of his congregation, St. Philip's. There were several drawbacks, though, which finally caused Sam to decide against the St. Louis seminary—the rigid language requirements, plus the added years at a preparatory school among students four or five years younger than he. Sam therefore chose the Springfield seminary.

It was in 1946 that both Samuel Hoard and I, his pastor, wrote the Springfield seminary of his intention to study for the ministry and his desire to attend that seminary. The president of the seminary, Dr. G. Christian Barth, wrote me in response: "This morning we had a faculty meeting and discussed the enrollment of Samuel Lawrence Hoard. I am very sorry to state that the faculty adopted a resolution to this effect: 'In view of our very large enrollment and furthermore in view of the fact that we have Immanuel College at Greensboro, North Carolina, for the training of colored men for the ministry, we cannot receive Mr. Hoard as one of our students.'"

Several attempts were made shortly thereafter to get the seminary faculty to change its position, but to no avail.

Lindsay Robinson, referred to previously, was also an ex-G.I. Being without employment after his discharge from the Army, he spent much of his time assisting in the work of the congregation. He too had been denied enrollment at the Springfield seminary. Jerry Wyatt, another ex-G.I., brother-in-law of the Rev. Clemonce Sabourin—a black Lutheran pastor in Harlem—was a convert to the Lutheran Church and wanted to study for the ministry. Pastor Sabourin wrote to the Springfield seminary on behalf of Mr. Wyatt's enrollment; he also phoned the seminary president, all to no avail. Othneil Thompson of New Orleans, whose father was a Lutheran pastor, was enrolled at the Springfield seminary. He came there with an M.A. in his hands, evidence of a much higher academic standing than that required by the seminary at that time and higher than that of most of the students enrolled there. Somehow the seminary had acted contrary to its established rule, for Mr. Thompson was a Negro. But the "mistake" was soon corrected: Mr. Thompson was told that the seminary would not receive him. He too was referred to the segregated school in North Carolina.

In the fall of 1947, shortly after I had moved to Chicago, the Rev. Edgar R. Pflug, who at that time was a member of the Northern Illinois District Missionary Board, and the Rev. Paul G. Amt, liaison missionary to the people of the Negro communities surrounding the big Missouri Synod churches of Fort Wayne, Indiana, and I, formed an ad hoc committee to meet with the board of control of the Springfield seminary. The meeting was held. We were given no evidence that the policy would be changed. The president of the institution who, incidentally, did all the talking for the board, made it quite clear that no change of policy would be effected in the near future.

In correspondence with the seminary president, as well as in telephone and face-to-face conversations, he stated repeatedly that the seminary's policy had no element of racial prejudice or discrimination in it; it was simply a matter of good, practical churchmanship: the Springfield seminary was overcrowded at the time; the Greensboro institution was in danger of going out of existence because it was able to attract so few young men who wanted to prepare for the ministry. Therefore the students in whose behalf we were speaking should go to Greensboro. It was as simple as that.

We thought it strange, though, and we told the president of the seminary and the board of control, that if racial prejudice or discrimination were not involved, why were Negroes singled out to be refused acceptance, and why didn't the president or the board, with the same persistency, direct Caucasian applicants to Greensboro and in doing so not only fill that institution with students but also free themselves from the opprobrium of racial discrimination?

In the same scholastic year that the Springfield seminary president and board of control refused to alter their position when the aforementioned committee asked them to do so, the seminary conferred the degree of Doctor of Divinity, *honoris causa*, on the Rev. Marmaduke Nathanael Carter, a Negro, pastor of St. Philip's Lutheran Church in Chicago. The degree was well deserved and was borne with proper dignity by the recipient. Conferring an honorary degree on a Negro while adamantly refusing to accept Negroes as students seemed to many of us to be quite inconsistent, if not hypocritical.

The name of Miss Rosa Young might well appear on the pages of Synodical Conference history and of The Lutheran Church-Missouri Synod as that of a consecrated and courageous pioneer missionary. She is the person who, under God, in 1916 was primarily responsible for the beginning and development of mission work in the black belt of Alabama. To the dismay of many informed people, though, a *Lutheran Witness* reporter in 1960 singled out Miss Young to ask her certain questions about the segregation issue.

She had spent her entire life in a backward part of her state, was well along in years (79), and had learned to adapt herself to living under the rigid segregation pattern of that place and time. Her answers to the questions addressed to her came out as could well have been anticipated. They bespoke the attitude of non-involvement of the church in this pressing issue. Miss Young's response was the kind segregationist-minded people in the church wanted. And it appeared that the *Witness* reporter concurred with Miss Young in her non-involvement stance. (Vol. 79, No. 1, Jan. 27, 1960, p. 7) Not long after the *Witness* article was published, tours were arranged for Miss Young to speak to Lutheran Women's Missionary League groups in different parts of the country, providing further exposure for her views.

Fifteen months later, after the full impact of the interview with Miss Young had taken place, Concordia Seminary, Springfield, Illinois, conferred on her the honorary degree of Doctor of Letters. Miss Young could in honesty and dignity bear this honorary title, and the conferral of the degree could well have enhanced the prestige of the seminary and served the church well; nevertheless, the conferral, coming at the time it did, was a mistake, according to the opinion of some, because it seemed to endorse the position of Miss Young.

About Concordia Teachers College, River Forest, Illinois

In 1935, in her late teens, Ruth Smith moved to Waukesha, Wisconsin with her mother. The impact of overt discrimination in education as it existed almost unchallenged before the 1954 Supreme Court desegregation decision was not only well-known to her; she had experienced it.

Let Miss Smith speak for herself. "There was a school within 50 yards of my home in Kentucky, but due to segregation laws I couldn't attend this school. Instead, I had to enroll in a segregated school five miles away. I either had to walk on a mere path or ride a mule to school, leaving home before daylight and arriving home after dark with only a kerosene lantern to light the way. Due to distance and bad weather I could go only a few months out of the year. I became discouraged and quit the school at the age of 17, though only in the sixth grade."

What was her experience after moving north, and how was she received by the church there?

The Lutheran Hour had brought her the message of a forgiving and loving God who for the redemption of the world gave His Son Jesus Christ into death. Miss Smith soon sought out the Lutheran church in Waukesha, and in 1941 became a member of a Wisconsin Synod church in that city. She told her pastor, the Reverend Harry Shiley, that she wanted to devote her life to the work of the church, and desired to continue her studies to that end.

Since Concordia Teachers College at River Forest, Illinois was a co-educational institution not far away, Pastor Shiley suggested that Miss Smith apply for admission. Her enrollment was arranged for by correspondence.

Pastor Shiley wrote me later that Ruth and her mother "went to River Forest in the fall of 1941. I got a long distance call from the director. He said I put him in an awful predicament; they could not take colored people. Send her to North Carolina. They came back brokenhearted. Mrs. Smith would not consider North Carolina because their standards were much lower down South."

Miss Smith experienced what I had tried to obviate for my parishioners in St. Louis when I wrote to St. Paul's College in Concordia, Missouri, as previously related.

Concordia Teachers College, maintained by The Lutheran Church-Missouri Synod, had reacted in keeping with the spirit of the times, a spirit that prevailed in society in general and in the church as well. It all happened quietly and "peacefully"; and the "order" that had been established for the lily-white suburban community had been maintained.

But what a blow it must have been to the sensitive spirit of the young woman! She was filled with the idealism of a dedicated young person and with love for the church she had only recently learned to know and to whose interest she wanted to dedicate her life. She was nevertheless rejected like an outcast by an institution that her church had established, rejected because of a God-given blessing—physical traits that helped to make of her a human being!

Miss Smith's pastor, perhaps to avoid deepening the wounds already inflicted, did not make a public issue of the offense committed against her; he simply phoned the institution of his own synod at New Ulm,

Minnesota. She was accepted and after three years was graduated.

Was Miss Smith "treated like a dog" by the institution that turned her away? Some may respond, and it would be hard to gainsay them, "She was treated worse than a dog." For it was in the summer of 1943 that I attended a class in child psychology at the same institution. Each day as members of the class assembled, a blind man entered the classroom guided by a dog. The dog would lie down in the aisle next to his master. Whether the dog got anything out of the lecture other than that his master was safe there, I do not know. But he was quiet; he disturbed no one and was disturbed by no one. In other words, he was accepted by the students, the instructor, and the institution.

In May 1970 Miss Smith concluded 25 years of teaching in the parochial school of Trinity Lutheran Church, Neenah, Wisconsin, a city where less than a dozen Negroes lived. She was lavishly honored at a testimonial dinner when the congregation gave ample evidence of their love and respect to a faithful servant of Christ.

A Cloud with a Silver Lining

But the times have changed; and Concordia Teachers College as well. Students at CTC have for many years and, more recently, in increasing numbers worked with all their youthful energy and in many capacities in Chicago's inner city Lutheran churches in predominantly black communities. The college itself has for some years now enrolled black students without discrimination, and had black professors on its faculty.

What became of those persons who were rejected by the Springfield seminary? Lindsay Robinson, as previously mentioned, was enrolled and studied at Concordia College, Milwaukee. Mr. Wyatt and Mr. Thompson were enrolled at and graduated from the institution at Greensboro. Mr. Hoard, after much difficulty because of his racial background, was enrolled at Concordia College, a preparatory school at Fort Wayne, and was graduated from the St. Louis seminary in 1957.

During the latter part of the fifties and the first years of the sixties I had occasion to visit, with one exception, all the educational institutions of The Lutheran Church-Missouri Synod, and to lecture at many of them. The impression I gained at the time was that they all (including the college at Austin, Texas) were consciously or otherwise vying with one another for the enrollment of black students. The Springfield seminary, since the beginning of the sixties, has been given ample opportunity to restore the better image it once had, and has not been found wanting.

The institution at Greensboro was closed, but the Alabama Lutheran Academy and College was not. In theory at least, the Alabama institution in previous years had been thought to be a feeder for the Greensboro seminary. Now that it was closed, the Springfield seminary seemed to be the logical institution for those studying at Selma and desiring to enter a seminary after their graduation. From then on and until this writing, the Springfield institution has enrolled and graduated more Negroes than all the other schools of higher learning of the Missouri Synod combined, the Selma school of course excepted.

During the sixties, Professor Paul G. Elbrecht was a member of the Springfield faculty. From what I was able to observe, he demonstrated by word and action the relevance of the good news in Jesus Christ for the church in the area of social responsibility, specifically race relations. He later accepted the unenviable job of president of Alabama Lutheran Academy and College in Selma, Alabama, and against great odds worked manfully to make that institution fit into the new picture of a fast-changing society.

Chapter Two

Are Parochial Schools the Answer?

F. C. D. Wyneken, referred to as one of the master builders of the Missouri Synod, is said to have questioned the advisability of the church's establishing parochial schools. If he were with us today, what would he say about founding and maintaining such schools?

Parochial Schools in Springfield, Illinois

True to solid Missouri Synod tradition in the first quarter of the twentieth century, and probably encouraged by the presence and influence of Concordia Seminary in Springfield, four of the five Missouri Synod churches of that town have developed and are maintaining strong parochial schools. At this writing the four schools employ a total of 25 teachers. The one congregation in Springfield that does not maintain a parochial school is Holy Trinity, the small congregation of predominantly Negro membership, of which I was the pastor from 1924 to 1928.

For decades it had been a policy followed quite generally by congregations maintaining parochial schools to invite children of non-members to attend. Among the non-members invited, those children who were members of another Missouri Synod congregation which had no school of its own were given priority. In keeping with sound evangelical principles, the parochial school was maintained in the first place to nurture the children of the congregation in Christian faith and piety. In the second place, the school was considered a mission agency, an arm to reach out into the community with the wholesome provender of the gospel to those who needed it most. But in doing so, and in keeping with an apostolic injunction, "especially those of the household of faith" were to receive first consideration.

With the exception of Trinity Church, Holy Trinity is the oldest church in Springfield with Missouri Synod roots; it had its origin as a preaching station in 1883. It may be difficult to find out how often members of Holy Trinity tried to enroll their children in the Missouri Synod parochial schools during the many years of its existence. One might well suppose that such applications would have been made, since Holy Trinity too must have learned by one means or another of the importance the Missouri Synod placed on Christian education in parochial schools.

Another assumption might well be made that the Missouri Synod churches of the city maintaining parochial schools, and the professors of the Springfield seminary who tried to inculcate in their students zeal for the parochial school, would have made it a point to have the children of the small mission congregation, Holy Trinity, enrolled at Trinity School and later in other Missouri Synod schools established in the city.

The psychology that kept me, when I was pastor of Holy Trinity, from confronting Trinity and Immanuel—the only Missouri Synod churches in the city at that time which maintained parochial schools—with the challenge of accepting the children of my parish, was the same psychology that kept them from inviting the children of Holy Trinity to attend. It was not merely a psychology. It was a psychology based on the prevailing theology. It emphasized the preaching of the gospel to help people get to heaven, with the result that social issues rumbling beneath the surface were conveniently circumvented. What is more, the admission or non-admission into the parochial school of Negro children of the same profession of faith was dismissed as irrelevant to the church's work because it was considered "a social question."

Not long after I became the pastor of Holy Trinity congregation I was "influential" in starting a one-room parochial school. It was "accomplished" with the help and advice of members of the seminary faculty, a small additional allowance from the Synodical Conference Missionary Board, and the weak approval of the congregation itself. When the doors of the school were opened, none of the leading members of the congregation sent their children. Almost all of those enrolled were from non-member homes.

As I learned later, the opening of a parochial school under the circumstances was a serious mistake. In this instance I was following the Missouri Synod "party line" as others were doing.

Although Springfield at the time fell far short of living up to the ideals often attributed to Abraham Lincoln (who had lived there), it did not maintain a system of school segregation. There was a fairly large concentration of Negroes in the area of Holy Trinity Church at that time, but the Negro population of the town was well scattered through the city. And there seemed to be no gerrymandering of school districts. When the Holy Trinity parochial school was about to be opened, several members of the congregation told me that they did not want to send their children to a segregated school; and that is what Holy Trinity parochial school for all practical purposes was. We could not integrate the school by enrolling our son; he was an infant at the time. As I recall, the members did not oppose the opening of the school, thinking as I did that it would be a missionary activity.

Instead of trying to establish a parochial school under such circumstances, I should have taken steps toward integrating the existing Lutheran schools. Step one would have been to teach the members of Holy Trinity the rightness of such integration, that they owed it to themselves, their community, the church at large, and especially their fellow Lutherans of the other Missouri Synod parishes. Since my members had a fairly good knowledge of the Scriptures, any one of a number of Scripture passages that speak of the unity of the church, if applied, might well have moved them to God-pleasing action. It is altogether possible that when confronted with all the facts, the fires of a holy and just indignation might have been kindled. It would have been all to the good.

A second step might have been that of confronting the other two congregations in question. At this point a tug-of-war could have ensued. (The pastor of the big congregation, Paul Schulz, at one time suggested that "a mild form of slavery might be the answer to the race problem.") The other congregation, Immanuel, which was really an offshoot of Trinity, was started as a parochial school project; and the pastor, the Rev. George R. Klein, had been installed the same year that the ill-fated Holy Trinity school was opened. As a seminarian he had worked at Holy Trinity.

What a forward-looking venture the enrollment of my school children in the already established parochial schools could have been! The disgrace of racial segregation in the church would have been obviated at least to some degree; the young seminary students would have had a classic model after which they could pattern their professional lives; the seminary faculty would have been provided a real workshop, taking them beyond theorizing on unity in the church to a living example of such unity; the congregations involved and especially the children of the churches would have experienced a sort of foretaste of heaven. Perhaps, too, little Holy Trinity congregation (now more than 75 years old) would have received a blood transfusion that would have kept it from merely vegetating—a problem to all involved, especially to the Missionary Board which had to supply the funds for a project that over decades had no doubt proved to them an unprofitable mission investment. Another and even happier turn of events might well have developed: the small struggling mission congregation, within easy walking distance of the churches with parochial schools, could have been led to merge with its neighbors, to the strengthening of both—spiritually, numerically, and financially.

Some were at that time already beginning to say that I was "twenty-five years ahead of the times" in what I said and did in the area of race relations. It was nevertheless due to my ineptness, coupled with a weak, other-worldly theology like that of the Lutheran clergy of the area, that Holy Trinity parochial school was begun, and the alternative discussed above, with all its potential for good, was not put into practice. "Lord, remember not the sins of my youth" (Ps. 25:7).

St. Louis: "To Whom Much is Given"

Missouri Synod Lutheranism in St. Louis, where many of the founders and leaders of the Synod lived and worked, was no exception to the rule: the Christian day school was considered the best agency to indoctrinate children and to make of them staunch members of the church, with all attendant blessings for the local congregation and for the church at large.

When I moved to St. Louis in 1928 to become the pastor of St. Philip's Church, there were 28 Missouri Synod congregations within the city limits; 18 of them had established Christian day schools; other such schools were later to come into existence. One of the churches with a Christian day school was Grace Mission located in the inner city. Its members, like the majority of the residents of the community, were Negroes. Begun in 1903, Grace Mission conducted a Christian day school almost from its inception. During its history many faithful and intelligent men and women, whose services elsewhere were greatly needed, served at Grace Mission, primarily through the day school; and money, no doubt running into the tens of thousands of dollars, was poured into this project.

Located near Grace Mission was Immanuel Church which had a day school. Dr. Franz August Otto Pieper, the president of Concordia Seminary, who for some time was also president of The Lutheran Church-Missouri Synod, was a member of that congregation. It is conceivable that this congregation—if it had had a relevant theology, and if its members had been conditioned by it to accept people without regard for class and race—might well have absorbed those who were to be ministered to through Grace Mission. It didn't happen though.

Grace Mission never had anything even remotely resembling a church edifice until 1927 when a new church building was erected at Goode & St. Ferdinand Avenues. The church and the congregation that was to worship there were renamed St. Philip's.

Shortly thereafter, Immanuel Church moved dangerously close to the new St. Philip's Church. (Since then it has moved once again.) If this "moving" church had in the beginning ministered to the people to whom Grace Mission ministered, it might well have been that St. Philip's would never have come into existence.

30

Before the turn of the century Holy Cross School of St. Louis enrolled at least one Negro. When I met her many years later, she was perhaps in her sixties. She had learned German at the school and was able to converse very well in German. Missouri Synod Christian day schools begun in the 19th century were German schools; religion and in many cases other subjects were taught in that language. Perhaps it took a great deal of courage on the part of those German-speaking Lutherans to invite and to welcome a non-German-speaking child to their school; and it required an equal amount of courage for non-German-speaking parents to accept the invitation for their children.

Another circumstance which might have helped to keep Negro children from enrolling in Missouri Synod parochial schools even after the language barrier had been removed was a state school-segregation law that prevailed in those days.

Since my sons were classified as white and I could not, according to the law, enroll them in a Negro school, we enrolled them in a nearby all-white Missouri Synod school. The fact that this law could not be applied to parochial schools was probably unknown to me as well as to my members at the time. This was in the thirties when racial tensions were emerging throughout the land. It was an open secret that the church's voice was not being heard at that time, espousing the cause of "the poor and needy." What I should have done was to challenge the churches of St. Louis to open the doors of their schools. And if Bethany School, which my children attended, did not open its doors to invite the children of my congregation, I should have withdrawn my own in open protest.

Even though some of my friends said I was ahead of the times in my race relations attitude, in the minds of many church leaders I had become suspect. Through lectures and articles written for certain periodicals, I had called upon the church to break down the racial barriers that had been built up unholily in the church. This led some of the Lutheran pastors of St. Louis to think that I was behind every move to change the status quo.

When an occasional Negro, taking the Lutheran Hour message seriously and seeing a Lutheran Hour sign in front of a church, attended a service, I was thought to have sent him. To check this unwarranted criticism (or praise, depending on how it is interpreted), I decided not to suggest to my members that they try to enroll their children in Lutheran day schools; I hoped that they would take that step on their own initiative. None of them did.

The closest that I at this time came to encouraging my members personally to attempt to break the racial barrier in the churches may be found in the answer I gave to some of my teenage young people. They asked for permission to attend the early service of nearby Grace Lutheran church some Sunday morning. They promised to hurry back to their own church to attend Bible class. I assured them of my approval. Grace Church whose services they attended on that occasion has since moved into the suburbs and has sold its property in the city—which would cost about $500,000 to replace—for $50,000.

By the time our youngest son was of high school age, a Missouri Synod Lutheran high school had been opened. We decided to enroll him and at the same time encouraged another boy of his age, a member of our congregation, to enroll. That was in 1946. Upon my return from California, where I had gone for a rest on advice of my doctor, the whole family and several members of my congregation met me at the railway station. They had exciting but disturbing news for me: the boy of our congregation had applied for enrollment at the Lutheran high school but was rejected because of his racial identity.

They reported to me all that had happened: how our eldest son, who was that year to enter the St. Louis Concordia Seminary, had consulted a trusted friend of mine, the Rev. Paul G. Amt; how upon his advice they confronted the high school authorities with the theological implications of the issue; and when they refused to change their decision Margaret had withdrawn our son's enrollment. I consulted the high school authorities. The principal, Dr. Paul W. Lange, told me that one influential member of the school's board of directors, a millionaire, was the one who held out to the last against admitting the boy from my congregation. Dr. Lange assured me, though, that the school would be open to Negroes at the beginning of the next school year.

"Place of an Evil Smell"—Chicago

Long before our lakes and streams were polluted by industry, even before there was any industry on the shoreline of Lake Michigan where that great metropolis called Chicago is to be found today, wild garlic was growing in great abundance. Though the garlic was more attractive to the eye than the shoreline of many of our polluted lakes and rivers today, it must have affected adversely the olfactory nerves of the Indians who lived nearby. Hence they called those shores "Chicago"— "the place of an evil smell." The garlic and its evil smell have long ago disappeared, but the name remains; and it has not lost altogether its original connotation.

Though River Forest is not within the municipality of Chicago, it is an adjoining suburban community. Concordia Teachers College of River Forest saw fit to deny Miss Ruth Smith enrollment because she was a

Negro; the same school, during the same decade and until I came to Chicago in 1947, tried to establish a mission congregation on Chicago's South Side, in the Negro community, by first establishing a Christian day school. The college was supported in its effort by the Mission Board of the Northern Illinois District of the Missouri Synod. Because of a lack of facilities, however, the mission school breathed its last breath approximately one year after I came to Chicago. Several years later, a family that was identified with the mission that survived the death of the mission school moved farther south in the city and within walking distance of St. Stephen's Lutheran Church and day school. The parents asked me to inquire into the possibility of enrolling their eldest child in the school.

The South Side Negro community of Chicago was expanding, moving farther south and west. The immediate community in which the church and school in question were found was still almost exclusively white, although some Negroes were now only several blocks to the north. The futile effort to stem the tide of community change was still being made, and the pastor of the congregation, the Rev. Oscar Fedder, in typical response to my inquiry concerning the enrollment of the child, told me, "We must cooperate with the community." The child was not enrolled because of race. But the "cooperation" was in vain. Not only did Negroes move into the whole area surrounding the church and school, but the school was closed not long thereafter; and later the school building itself was razed. Today, at least in part because of the congregation's "cooperation" to keep Negroes away, the congregation is but a shadow of its former self.

The Rev. Erwin H. Meinzen, missionary on leave from India, was acting as interim pastor at First Immanuel on the near southwest side of Chicago. The church was vegetating, serving its own members, the great majority of whom had long ago moved to the suburbs or to other parts of the city where they were far removed from its inner-core problems and challenges. The church was living out the last few years of its century-old existence. But it was now seemingly complacent, unmindful of the people living in the immediate environs of the church, first generation Mexicans, Puerto Ricans, Greeks, Italians, yes, and Negroes as well. The community was truly interracial and cosmopolitan, as few places in the United States.

Pastor Meinzen must have been conscious of the utter necessity of community outreach in his work in India for his mission's life and justification—the very reason for his having spent 20 years there and for his returning to that country. Had he taken, though for a few short months,

33

a responsibility inimical to his whole past professional life? Could he serve First Immanuel without getting at the gut issue—its responsibility to the community in which many were in as great a need as the poorest pariah in India? And how could he do it without stirring up a hornet's nest of bitter opposition?

At the time, I was still pastor of St. Philip's Church in St. Louis, but was to make several trips to Chicago. Pastor Meinzen, a friend of mine, asked me to stop by to talk over the dilemma confronting him. After we had talked at some length, he suggested that we would go to the day school and speak to the upper classes.

How could I talk to these boys and girls, ten to fourteen years old, on the matter for which I had come, without myself doing the first stirring of the hornet's nest? As I had often before addressed Sunday schools of churches of all-white constituency, I asked the children, if they had their choice, which of two flower gardens they would like best, one with white flowers only or one with flowers of many colors. The response was what was anticipated; they liked the garden with flowers of many colors. Then I told them that it is God's desire for his church on earth that people of all colors and nationalities were to be brought into His church, to enjoy together the good news about Jesus the Savior. A twelve-year-old boy, with the forthright candor common to children, asked me why there were no Negro or Italian children in their day school.

Fort Wayne Parochial School Integration

One of the best examples of integration in Missouri Synod Christian day schools was that of Fort Wayne, Indiana. In the middle of the forties the Missouri Synod Lutheran community somehow suddenly awoke to the realization that its churches in the city, a number of them quite large, with big, well-established parochial schools, were in areas where many Negroes were now living. Few if any of the newcomers were identified with the Lutheran church.

The Rev. Paul G. Amt was called to work in the community. (A close friend of mine, he kept in touch with me during his entire ministry in Fort Wayne.) He was given the privilege of establishing his own approach for the church in its outreach to the Negroes living there. Pastor Amt had an unusually clear understanding of the needs of the day, and a theology that did not bypass the unity of all believers in the church as well as in the body of Christ. Honestly facing the reality of the close proximity of the churches to the Negro population of the city, he asked the Missouri Synod pastors of the town for their full cooperation while he would work as a liaison between the churches and the people of the community. He told them he would move about in the community and, as opportunity presented itself, witness to Christ and extend to those with whom he came into favorable contact the warm welcome of the churches and the hearty invitation for them to send their children to the Lutheran day schools of the city.

Pastor Amt was promised freedom of movement. But because his approach was radically different from the usual way of working among Negroes until that time, the steps he took were at first looked upon with great skepticism by some and resisted by others.

Pastor Amt's immediate and most effective ministry was gaining children for the established Christian day schools; twenty-three were enrolled in several of the schools during his ministry. Adults, too, though not many, became members of several congregations during Pastor Amt's ministry, largely through the liaison work he carried on. In a sense, it is surprising that his efforts proved to be as successful as they did in view of the fact that Lutheranism was something completely new to the great majority of Negroes in Fort Wayne and that the Lutherans of . Fort Wayne, previous to the coming of Pastor Amt, seemed to have ignored their presence.

After several years of hard work on the part of Pastor Amt, and when the full fruits of his labors might well have been anticipated, some leaders grew impatient. They urged the establishment of a new mission right in the center of a circle of Lutheran churches. It was to be a "cosmopolitan" church. When this plan was urged upon the churches and adopted, Pastor Amt felt that his work in Fort Wayne was finished. And since he did not favor the plan of establishing a new church in the community, albeit it was to be spoken and thought of as a "cosmopolitan" church, he accepted a call elsewhere.

The "cosmopolitan" church was begun. But that is another story. Our present concern is to call attention to the liaison type of ministry that was established and the promise of a theologically sound approach to effective work through established Christian day schools and churches.

Whip of God upon the Church

In the Plessy-Ferguson decision of 1896, the Supreme Court of the United States declared in substance that racial segregation in public transportation, if it is "separate but equal," was not contrary to the Constitution, the supreme law of the land. This decision gave legal status and sanction—or thus it was interpreted—to segregation in every possible phase of public life.

The rule was adhered to rigidly by the courts in the South and the courts' decisions were upheld and supported by public opinion, both verbalized and lived out in all aspects of public social contact. In the North, segregation was not as overt as in the South, but with the migration of millions of Negroes from the South to the North and West, many ways were devised by white society to impose segregation on its communities without taking recourse to the "separate but equal" decision.

Another Supreme Court pronouncement destined to change the course of U.S. history was the Brown v. Board of Education decision of May 17, 1954. (For a brief survey of pertinent decisions of the Supreme Court, see *Fire from the Throne*, St. Louis, Mo., Concordia Publishing House, 1968, pp. 46-49; and for a more detailed review of racial segregation, see *The Strange Career of Jim Crow*, Oxford University Press, 1957). In substance the 1954 decision annulled the Plessy-Ferguson decision and all other decisions that would give legal status to segregation.

Before 1954, church-schools desiring to practice racial inclusion might have claimed that private schools were not commanded by law to segregate. Perhaps the opposite can be said since 1954: private schools are not compelled by state or Federal law to integrate, i.e., to abolish segregation.

Before the 1954 Supreme Court decision, the Missouri Synod with hundreds of parochial schools—some of them in the South—went along complacently living within the framework of the racial status quo, neither advocating, at least verbally, racial segregation in its schools, nor challenging segregation in its own or other schools. But the die was now cast. Missouri Synod members on both sides of the racial fence in their thinking, and the hundreds of thousands who until now had given the matter little thought, would either want or need some expression by synodical officials that could help give them guidance in thought and action.

Dr. John W. Behnken, president of the Missouri Synod, called a meeting to discuss the matter. The meeting was held, perhaps primarily, for the officers of those synodical districts thought to be most directly involved, whose geographic boundaries included the 17 Southern states. At least some of those who attended were competent and theologically awake as well as understanding of the times. Although the weal or woe of black people was involved in the subject matter discussed, no black person was in attendance. Dr. Henry F. Wind, probably anticipating this situation, brought with him a statement prepared by the Rev. Mr. Sabourin, pastor of Mount Zion Lutheran Church in Harlem. The statement was read, and thus, at least vicariously, one black person had something to say at the meeting.

Dr. Oswald C. J. Hoffmann, Lutheran Hour speaker, and at that time the Director of Public Relations of The Lutheran Church-Missouri Synod, was in attendance. According to the minutes of the meeting, he stated "that the pressure on the Public Relations Department is terrific to have a statement of the attitude of our synod on this matter." The minutes tell us further that "Dr. Behnken was asked to appoint the committee that is to formulate this general policy [with reference to school integration]. He is also to publish a statement on this meeting, including the idea that a committee was being appointed."

The minutes of the meeting state further that "the secretary agreed to send a report of the meeting, including a copy of the various papers presented, to all participants."

When preparing this part of the manuscript, I wrote Dr. Martin H. Scharlemann who read a paper at the meeting, asking him if he knew of any public statement having been made with reference to the meeting and its findings. He responded, "Dr. Behnken did not appoint the committee he was asked to establish. All that came out was my statement published in the Concordia Theological Monthly" (25:615-19, August 1954). Whatever of value might have been derived from the meeting was apparently never made known publicly to the Synod. And, again, no guidance for clergy and laity was forthcoming.

In a minor and perhaps indirect way the meeting probably bore some fruit; at least some of those in attendance must have had their theological swords sharpened to prepare them for the battle then in the offing, but far from being resolved even at this writing.

A great evil has been committed by our nation against a people "who are different from the rest of us in skin color only" (and that distinction, by the way, is a part of the handiwork of God Himself). There should be no doubt in the minds of those who believe that God is, that the Brown v. Board of Education decision of 1954, with all the turmoil that has developed since, is *God's whip upon our nation*. It is that, and more. *It is also and primarily God's whip upon the church* of our nation; it is God's chastening rod. And since the Supreme Court decision is centered in the school system of the nation, and church schools are at least theoretically intended to prepare the coming generation for the years that lie immediately ahead, some in the church are trying to take an honest new look at the parochial schools as they ask the questions: Are these schools, in their present structure, serving church and nation well? Can the system itself be so altered, if necessary, as to justify its continued existence? Or should the parochial school fade out of existence, like something old that has perhaps served a good purpose but is of value today only as a memory to be preserved in history books for scholars of the future to study?

These questions are being asked within both American church bodies that maintain the greatest number of parochial schools, The Lutheran Church-Missouri Synod and, of course, the Roman Catholic Church. (The heading of this chapter, "Are Parochial Schools the Answer?" is the title of a book written by a Roman Catholic woman, Mary Perkins Ryan. The book questions the validity of Roman Catholic schools. A similar study which questions the advisability of maintaining parochial schools in The Lutheran Church-Missouri Synod was made by Ronald L. Johnstone who at the time he made the study was on the faculty of Concordia Seminary in St. Louis.)

The examples of policies and attitudes of parochial schools within The Lutheran Church-Missouri Synod as described on the foregoing pages are a part, but only a part, of the body of reference for an honest and relevant evaluation of the parochial school system which has been in existence within the Missouri Synod for many decades.

Another element of fact, more basic to the conclusion which I am about to advance than the foregoing examples of attitudes and policies, is the theology of The Lutheran Church-Missouri Synod of the early years of this century. In its overemphasis on the eternal salvation of the soul, the Missouri Synod, in common with other church bodies, negated, neglected, or even considered invalid the concern for man's temporal and physical well-being beyond a gesture of interest in the area of social welfare. The reformation of society as such, for example, was considered a matter of theological or ecclesiastical indifference.

With this theological background, there is little wonder that the Missouri Synod and other church bodies of a similar theological heritage were wont to say, even in the face of immediate crying need for a basic change in our society, "Just preach the gospel; that will take care of it." But this type of "preaching the gospel" and teaching it did *not* "take care of it." Race relations continued with little marked change for the better. *Those who were taught the gospel in our parochial schools*—and this is the most charitable conclusion that can be drawn—*were no more involved, and often less, than those without such teaching, in working toward the eradication of racism in our midst.*

Perhaps there are statistics available giving the number of members of The Lutheran Church-Missouri Synod who at the time of the Supreme Court decision of May 17, 1954, had been trained in its parochial schools. It is evident, though, that with hundreds of parochial schools functioning at that time—and a greater percentage of congregations with such

38

schools than at this writing—hundreds of thousands of Missouri Synod members were the products of parochial schools and perhaps an even larger percentage of its pastors, parochial school teachers and synodical officials were products of its own cherished school system.

To undergird the foregoing statement—that "those who were taught the gospel in our parochial schools . . . were no more involved, and often less, than those without such teaching, in working toward the eradication of racism in our midst"—reference shall be made here merely to one aspect of one event in Missouri Synod history: the issuing of its first race relations pronouncement.

The predecessor of the World Council of Churches, at its Oxford Conference in 1937, adopted a good and forthright race relations pronouncement which was to set the tone for others soon to follow. A similar pronouncement was adopted in 1946 by the Federal Council of Churches of Christ in America, the predecessor of the National Council of the Churches of Christ in America. All the major denominations in this country soon followed suit; also the United Lutheran Church in America and the American Lutheran Church. The Lutheran Church-Missouri Synod was the last of the major church bodies to speak out on this vital issue. It happened in 1956, and it is mentioned here to emphasize its lateness.

Under the ultra-conservative theology of the Missouri Synod, its Christian day schools helped in a big way to develop its thought pattern as well as its action or non-action. It is fair, therefore, to assume that the lateness of the Missouri Synod in coming out publicly through a pronouncement on the race issue was at least in part a reflection of the influence of its parochial schools on the development or non-development of Christian social concern. *To understand, though, the conclusions to which I have come concerning the lack of a truly relevant Christian social concern, especially in the area of race in 1954 and to a great degree since then, the reader must take into consideration all aspects of the life and function of The Lutheran Church-Missouri Synod as described throughout this book.*

A Latent Potential for Good

We have thus far heaped much negative criticism on the Christian day school system of the Missouri Synod. The Christian day school nevertheless has a latent potential for good. There is within it the possibility for the development of a greater degree of Christian social concern as well as other virtues of Christian faith and life.

There is evidence in the recent curricular thrust and in other activities of both teacher training schools of the Synod (the Concordia Teachers

Colleges in River Forest, Illinois, and Seward, Nebraska) that these institutions have become conscious of the potential of the Christian day school and are now trying manfully to prepare their students for the challenge of developing the potential into reality.

Furthermore, there are now already such Christian day schools within the Missouri Synod that are, in their individual curricula and action programs, trying to generate a social consciousness in their pupils. This should be the natural outgrowth of a well-balanced theology which would help to prepare them for the challenging years ahead in which the church will live or die in keeping with its attitude toward the whole man, not only his soul.

It may be well at this juncture to call attention once again to the question raised by F. C. D. Wyneken concerning the advisability of the church's establishing day schools. His concern was that the chief responsibility for the Christian training of the child is not that of the church nor the school, but the home. Since Wyneken's time, psychologists have amply demonstrated the overwhelming influence of the home upon the child when compared with that of other agencies during the formative period of the child's life. If this is the case, the effect on the child's life even of the best conceivable Christian day school will be dependent to a large degree on the home environment and influence. If in the home there is an evident concern for better race relations, the home influence will greatly undergird what a good Christian day school will desire to do for the child. But a good Christian day school will nevertheless be seriously handicapped in its thrust toward the development in the child of a Christian social concern if the home is unconcerned; and if the home atmosphere is hostile, even the best efforts of the school may go down the drain

The problem confronting a Christian day school of The Lutheran Church-Missouri Synod in the concern of this section of the book is not the day school as such. It is rather the one-sided conservative theology of the past decades which kept congregations from awakening in their members a broad social awareness. This in turn led to non-involvement in matters that have a direct bearing on the well-being of society, a refusal to become involved in activities to reform a deformed society.

It would be equivalent to living in a fool's paradise to believe that Missouri Synod homes, at least until, say, 1954, were ready to give their wholehearted approval of and support to any endeavor of the Christian day school to develop a wholesome and very necessary social concern in the pupils of that school. With or without a Christian day school of the best type—from the viewpoint of Christian social concern—there is perhaps nothing short of a special social ministry, at least in the larger congregations of The Lutheran Church-Missouri Synod, which *would work in and with the home, to undo the harm that decades of moving along with the status quo has built up in its people.*

Chapter Three

Ecclesiastical Power Structure

A watchman for the house of Israel
Ezekiel 33:7

Confrontation with President of Synod

"I need not remind you that I am from south of the Mason-Dixon line. Brethren, it will never do," he said, and sat down. The occasion was the biennial convention of the Evangelical Lutheran Synodical Conference of North America assembled in Indianapolis, Indiana, in the summer of 1936. The statement was made by Dr. John W. Behnken, the recently elected president of The Lutheran Church-Missouri Synod, when a resolution had been presented that had to do with the Negro mission work conducted by the Synodical Conference.

This mission work had been carried on for almost 60 years. The congregations which were the outgrowth of the work—the great majority "south of the Mason-Dixon line"—were still financially dependent on the Synodical Conference.

The chief purpose of the Synodical Conference was "to express and confess the unity of the Spirit existing in the constituent synods; to give mutual aid and assistance toward the strengthening of their faith and confession; to promote, and preserve over against all disturbances, the unity in doctrine and practice . . . " (Lutheran Cyclopedia, p. 1030, 1954).

Presumably conceived in the womb of synodical unity and born and nurtured in Christian love, these Negro mission congregations, north and south, were members of none of the constituent synods of the Synodical Conference and therefore also not members of the Synodical Conference itself. They were at best step-children. Times were changing, though, for the church as well as the nation. In keeping with the times, a committee had been appointed to look into the matter and to report its findings to the convention. The committee's report was in the form of a resolution.

The resolution of the so-called floor committee recommended no earth-shaking change. There was no call to repentance for permitting these mission congregations to stand like rejected bastards on the outside, without personally experiencing the unity and the love that was the purpose of their having been conceived and born. The organizational-structure change that the committee asked for was equally mild. The resolution recommended that the two self-supporting congregations of predominantly Negro constituency—one in St. Louis and the other in Chicago, and therefore neither of them actually in the South—be advised to seek membership in the synodical districts in which they were located. The matter of the organic membership and therefore also the fellowship of all the rest of the congregations in question was to be held in abeyance until some future unspecified date.

The pastor of the Chicago congregation, the Rev. Marmaduke Nathanael Carter, was not present. I was the pastor of the St. Louis congregation. In keeping with the humility befitting or thought to befit one in so lowly a position as that in which I found myself, I was seated in the balcony in the rear of the church where the convention was being held.

When the chairman of the convention called upon the floor committee to make its report and recommendation, I quickly laid aside my humility, rushed downstairs, and seated myself among the important folk as though I were one of them. A committee member made his report and read the resolution. Several questions were asked of the committee and when they had been answered, the above-quoted words, "I need not remind you . . . it will never do," were spoken by the president of the Missouri Synod.

When I found that no one was going to respond in defense of at least the little good contained in the resolution—a first though weak step toward the recognition of the brotherhood of the congregations involved —I asked for the floor, and got it.

I pointed to the inconsistency of our past performance and its detrimental effect on the mission work we purportedly wanted to do. A denial of Christ was also involved, I said, who came to us in our Negro brothers and sisters; for by denying them the fellowship in the church which we extended freely to others of the same profession of faith, we were denying it to Christ Himself.

As often happens—not necessarily with malice aforethought—highly controversial matters are not discussed by conventions until they are nearing adjournment. In this case, the resolution in question was brought to the floor immediately before adjournment for lunch.

The president of the Missouri Synod had spoken, and over 80 percent of the delegates were members of that Synod. No one else having asked for the floor, the motion was called, and the resolution was rejected. At

43

least another two years had to pass with this vital question remaining in limbo.

The delegates began to file out of the church. Several friends stopped where I was standing and commented on what had just transpired. Then Dr. Behnken came by. He said he wanted to assure me that he was "a friend of the colored man." As evidence, he related the following anecdote. One of his sons had gone with him to attend Vespers in a church in Chicago. As the preacher for the evening ascended the pulpit, the boy whispered to him: "That's a nigger preacher." Evidently to impress on me that he was "a friend of the colored man," he repeated what he had told the boy: "Hush, he is one of our colored preachers."

The president continued talking in the same vein. When I did not respond, he must have assumed that I was ready for a short commentary on his remark made a few minutes earlier to the convention. He called me by name: "You know, Pastor Schulze, if you give a colored man a little, he will want everything." It was a repetition of a stereotype that I had heard many times before and a form of degradation of many Spirit-filled Christians, Negroes all, whose shoes I am not worthy to polish.

My response was calm but nonetheless sharp: "Isn't your statement a denial of the power of the gospel?" Whether my answer came directly from the stronghold of the "father of lies" or whether it was motivated by the Holy Spirit, I shall not try to answer here.

There can be no doubt about the heresy involved in the president's remark, "give a colored man a little and he will want everything." A similar remark had often been made by segregationists, both south and north of the Mason-Dixon line and was used by them to imply that if civil rights and freedom in general were allowed Negroes, "they" would then want their black sons to marry "our" white daughters. But what made the stereotype so reprehensible was the context in which it was used in this instance. The question involved was the right of Negroes of the same confession to enter into organic union with the church body or bodies that had been used by the Spirit of God to cause them to make that confession. The stereotype implied that there are certain rights and privileges as well as responsibilities in the church that are not intended for all.

My reply made, the conversation ended abruptly.

Dr. Behnken had on more than one occasion previous to his election to the synodical presidency revealed in clear, unmistakable terms that he had imbibed some of his Texas compatriots' segregationist spirit. E.g., when the Friendship Society of Holy Trinity congregation in Springfield, Illinois, in 1922 had been accepted into membership of the Central Illinois District of the Walther League, a letter of vigorous protest was sent by the Texan who in about another decade was to become the president of the Missouri Synod.

Dr. Behnken wrote the Executive Board of the International Walther League on April 27, 1922 in part as follows: "Far more prominence than the matter calls for has been given to the acceptance of this society, even more than to the acceptance of ten or twelve white societies. Now, we readily understand that the North regards this to be a distinct triumph, and looks upon it as a mere beginning of greater results in this particular field in the future. . . . You may think us to be quite bigoted, narrow-minded, and erratic for opposing such a move in the Walther League circles. . . . When such matters once become public property, your Southern friends will be made to feel the sting of this social equality between whites and blacks. . . . If this matter is not rectified in some way, or if further Negro societies will be received into the league, it will eventually mean the withdrawal of all Walther Leagues below the Mason and Dixon line. . . . As far as mission work among the Negroes is concerned, our Southern people try to do their part, but we know that it is absolutely impossible for us to sanction social equality."

The Texas pastor was a dynamic preacher, aflame with evangelistic zeal. It was primarily through his vigorous leadership that The Lutheran Church-Missouri Synod was, so to speak, put on the map in Texas. This had its impact on the Synod as a whole. Whether or not they knew or were concerned about his segregationist spirit, the Missouri Synod delegates to the convention in Indianapolis knew that he had brought success to the efforts of the church in Texas; and if he could do it there, he could help that it be done throughout the area of the Synod's work, a very practical reason for his having been elected to the highest office of the Synod.

During the crucial years that followed his first election, when race was an important element of the criteria by which the church was to be judged by people of understanding and good will, the president, who was re-elected eight times, was very slow in moving toward a viewpoint that is truly reflective of the spirit of the Head of the church, of whom the Letter to the Hebrews says, "He is not ashamed to call them his brothers" (2:11, Phillips Translation).

When a more forthright expression in word and deed of what is Christian in race relations was required, Dr. Behnken would ask for restraint. On many occasions he would deplore what he called "agitating." When he felt strongly about a certain issue that was being discussed on the floor of synodical conventions, he would ask one of the Synod's vice-presidents to take the chair, while he would present to the delegates in

45

his forthright, unequivocal and persuasive manner his personal viewpoint. To my knowledge, not once, however, did he take up the cause of the black man in our midst, as we are enjoined to do by the Old Testament seer, "Open your mouth for the dumb, for the rights of all who are left desolate. Open your mouth, judge righteously, maintain the rights of the poor and needy" (Prov. 31:8-9). Dr. Behnken was nevertheless a child of God who wrought much good for the church and who, we trust, is now numbered among the saints in everlasting glory. What a happy inconsistency! May the same grace be extended me.

Dialogue on Strategy and Principle

Having burned my fingers often before at the too warm fires of mission boards, I had become careful if not cagy. At the time, I had 23 years in the pastoral ministry behind me; and now I had received a call from the Northern Illinois District of The Lutheran Church-Missouri Synod to become what for all practical purposes was a missionary-at-large for Chicago's South Side with its hundreds of thousands of Negroes and with only one Missouri Synod church serving them.

Before making a decision concerning the call, I proposed to the mission board of the district that I would come to Chicago to discuss with them both strategy and the principle on which the strategy should be based. Upon their invitation I met with them. At this first meeting we discussed strategy: where to begin new work; what to do about a vegetating mission which had been begun some 10 years previously but had proved to be not too successful according to a number of criteria; where and when new missionaries were to be called into the field, and where and when new chapels should be erected. There was seemingly little disagreement as to the strategy to be followed.

I had deep convictions about certain theological guidelines or principles with reference to the church's approach to dealing, working, and living with people of a racial background different from that of the majority within the church. Before I could work with a degree of harmony with the mission board in question, and they with me, I felt that a frank discussion of this matter would help me to make an intelligent and God-pleasing decision as to the call I was then considering.

It was the spring of 1947. My book, *My Neighbor of Another Color* (a treatise on race relations in the church), had been published five years earlier; from 1930 to 1946 I had been the president of the General Conference of workers in the "Negro Mission" of the Synodical Conference; I was a member of the St. Louis Mayor's Commission on Race Relations; chief organizer of the St. Louis Lutheran Society for Better Race Relations and editor of its monthly paper, the *Lutheran Race Re-*

lations Bulletin. I had written a number of articles on the subject of race for the *Walther League Messenger,* the *American Lutheran,* and other publications; and I was a member of the Missionary Board of the Synodical Conference.

The members of the Northern Illinois District Mission Board no doubt had more than an inkling of what my thinking was and what I had done in the field of race relations; it could not have gone unnoticed by them. Since there were other items on the agenda of the meeting I attended, I was invited to meet with them again when I could discuss with them at greater length the implications of the race issue for the church.

At the second meeting I outlined what I at the time considered a relevant theology for the church in the area of race relations. When I had finished, and after a few moments of silence, the secretary of missions of the district, the Rev. Arnold H. Semmann spoke. In unsophisticated candor he said, "I understand your viewpoint although I do not agree with you." After I had answered a number of questions, the chairman of the board said what seemed to be the consensus, that it would be my privilege to speak on the matter of race as my conscience dictated. With that assurance I returned to St. Louis and shortly thereafter accepted the call to Chicago.

The Battle is Joined

It wasn't long after we moved to Chicago that I began to receive and accept invitations to preach in some of the many churches of the Missouri Synod in Chicago and its environs and to lecture at meetings of congregational and church auxiliaries. One of the earliest invitations was to preach on "Mission Festival Sunday" at St. Peter's Church on Chicago's South Side. Some 10 or 15 years earlier this church had moved to its present location from an area farther north when Negroes began to move into that community. The replacement value of the congregation's new premises, which included the church edifice, a parochial school building, and a parsonage was about $500,000. Two Negro families had already moved into the area. I am not sure that I knew these facts before I preached there, since it was my custom not to ask many questions about a given congregation's history, etc., so that I could preach as objectively and dispassionately as possible.

When asked to preach, I almost invariably used either the Epistle or the Gospel lection for the Sunday as the text for the sermon. This, I thought, helped me to preach relevantly in keeping with the church year; and since I saw the message I had to proclaim [concerning the church's outreach toward people of a racial or ethnic background different from that of the dominant group in the church] in the Scriptures

47

in general and in the Epistles and Gospels in particular, the lections for a specific Sunday gave me opportunity to make the needed application without appearing to have a chip on my shoulder.

In keeping with this modus operandi, I addressed the South Side congregation in question on the work I was called to do in their midst and the mission challenge that it presented. The closest I came to directing a personal challenge to this specific congregation was a statement something to this effect: "I am sure that, as you pray for and give toward the work I am doing, if and when a Negro attends your church as a direct result of the Lutheran Hour or of my work on the South Side, you will freely and cordially welcome him." That was all.

After the service, when the pastor, the Rev. Arthur B. Preisinger, and I were removing our vestments in the sacristy, I noticed that, for one reason or another, he seemed to be somewhat nervous. On Wednesday of that week, Dr. Martin Piehler, the executive director of the Northern Illinois District, who was ex-officio a member of the district mission board, called me by phone. He wanted to comment on the word he had received concerning my sermon on the previous Sunday and its reception.

Rather than discuss such a delicate and, for me, personal question at any length over the phone, it was suggested that I should come to the district office at 77 W. Washington Street to discuss the matter with several members of the district executive staff. It was the first of many confrontations that were to take place in my seven years' sojourn in the Windy City. I may not have realized it at the time, but the meeting was in the nature of a straw in the wind pointing in the direction of a basic theological disparity involved in our working together.

The battle was joined; those with whom I met at the district office accepted the report they had received from others concerning my sermon and were in essential agreement with their informers; and I was asked to desist from "disturbing" congregations by preaching about or alluding to what I believed was a Christian response to the question of racial integration. How glad I was then and on similar occasions later when meeting with district officers or the district mission board, that I had, before accepting the call, discussed with them the race issue per se and that the consensus was that I should be free to discuss the issue in keeping with the dictates of my conscience.

After I had preached or lectured in many places throughout the district, Dr. Piehler informed me that at a meeting of the counselors of the district the content of my sermons and lectures had been severely criticized. I was told that I was "agitating," and in an injudicious manner disturbing the peace. Actually, my lectures and sermons were delivered only upon invitation, and I had the practice of telling those who invited me what I would talk about.

On one occasion I was invited by a group of Walther League societies to speak on the church and the race issue. At least one circuit counselor was present, besides the president of the district, the Rev. Carl L. Abel, in whose church the meeting was held. After he heard my lecture and the discussion that followed, Pastor Abel told me he would have invited his entire congregation to attend had he known the nature of my lecture. I mentioned this to the executive director when he informed me of the alleged complaint coming from the meeting of the counselors. I told him further that on no occasion had any counselor complained to me personally about the nature of my sermons and lectures, although many of them heard me speak on one or more occasions.

In order that at least a degree of justice be involved, the accused, I said, should have opportunity to appear before his accusers. To put it in evangelical terms, I suggested to the executive director that he speak to his complainants, telling them that I would be glad, upon their invitation, to attend a meeting of the counselors to discuss with them the content of my sermons and lectures delivered in their circuits. Whether my suggestion was transmitted to those for whom it was intended, I never found out. But the invitation never came through.

A Mission in the Church's Back Yard

The rent ceiling established as a wartime measure was still in effect when we moved to Chicago in August, 1947. The mission board had secured for us in advance of our coming a small three-room apartment at 928 E. 61st Street. During the vacation period, when all three of our sons were at home, our living quarters were quite inadequate. Our own home furnishings for seven rooms were put in storage at a cost to the mission board of $100 a month; and they were paying $90 a month for the "furnished" apartment. The sleeping facilities it offered were one Murphy bed and one double couch; there were several pieces of over-stuffed furniture with the stuffing coming out at the bottom, and two superannuated rugs so filthy that — well.

We offered the landlord that, with his consent, and without his lowering the rent, we would move some of his furniture and the rugs to any convenient storage place in the basement so that we could replace them with some of our own furnishings. The offer did not appeal to him, for then he could not have claimed it as a furnished apartment.

While the mission board placed upon us the responsibility of trying to find better living quarters, the board was concerned that it would happen. But to find and rent an apartment fit for human habitation in that part of over-crowded Chicago was like searching for the proverbial needle in the haystack.

After several months of fruitless searching on our part, the secretary of missions, the Rev. Arnold H. Semmann, called me one day. His voice was unusually cheerful. He had uncovered a real bonanza: an "apartment" in the school building of Gethsemane Church on the South Side that was available to us. Would I come to the Gethsemane parsonage on the same premises that evening to meet and to discuss with him, Dr. Piehler, and the Rev. Paul J. Eickstaedt (the pastor of Gethsemane) the possibility of our moving into this church-owned "apartment"?

The four of us met. After a few introductory remarks, it was decided to go to the school to see the apartment. The building was a frame structure built before the turn of the century, and had not been in use for many years. It reminded me in several ways of my grandfather's barn which had been razed some forty years earlier; and the rooms we had come to see brought back memories of the one room that adjoined the hayloft of grandfather's barn, in which he permitted any vagrant to take up his abode for the price of taking care of one horse and one cow.

The school building had one wide, squeaky stairway leading high above the first-floor classrooms to the apartment. There were no heating facilities. The walls and ceilings had not been decorated in many years and the floor was equally neglected.

In keeping with his usual optimistic spirit, Pastor Semmann was all aglow with the thought of the possibilities the apartment offered; and I, with a normal hankering for things more primitive, was not altogether untouched by the warmth of his enthusiasm.

After a number of suggestions had been made as to how the place could be made livable, it was decided to return to the parsonage for further discussion.

Back in the pastor's study in the parsonage, it was suggested, among other things, that, at the expense of the mission board—the congregation allowing the apartment to be used by me rent-free—the walls, ceilings, and floors would be painted, some new plumbing and two good oil-burning stoves installed. It was further suggested that, with the Schulze family well settled, who knows but what some Sunday school work could be started, thus making use of the unused school rooms; Negro children could be invited to come; and, one never could tell, a Negro mission congregation could in time result. (Except for a park on one side of the church premises, the community was populated almost exclusively by Negroes.)

Immediately I thought of a similar plan that was carried out some 15 years previously in Cleveland, Ohio, when Negroes had begun to move

50

into the community of St. Peter's Church of which the Rev. A. F. Katt was pastor. The Rev. Ernst G. Mueller, a graduate of Concordia Seminary, St. Louis, was called to begin Negro mission work in the community, and the school building to the rear of the church was used for the mission's Sunday school, church work, and services. The mission vegetated for about six years. By this time the residents of the community were mostly Negroes, the established congregation moved elsewhere, and the church property, through the financial assistance of the missionary board, was turned over to the mission congregation, St. Philip's. It was so stigmatized by its history of segregation, though, that the newcomers to the community never looked upon this church as something "for them," and after a few years the mission congregation itself moved out of the community.

While I was comparing in my mind what happened in Cleveland with what was now being suggested, Dr. Piehler turned to me and said quite abruptly, "Schulze, so far we have heard little or nothing from you. What do you have to say?" I was not only anticipating the question; I was ready to answer.

After a brief pause, I responded: "For a long time my family and I have gladly accepted many deprivations of life in the ministry and in mission work. Who among you, after 23 years of such a life, would want to move your family into those rooms above the school? Besides," I continued, "the plan to begin a Negro mission in the back yard of this congregation is unacceptable to me." I proceeded to tell them why, for pragmatic reasons alone, the plan would be out of the question, calling their attention to what had happened in Cleveland. My main reason, though, for rejecting the plan of trying to establish the proposed mission work was that it had segregation as its basis, which was contrary to the theology I set forth in my early meeting with the district mission board. The district executives were well aware of this.

With that said, I suggested an alternate plan: "I will move my family into the school apartment, if it is agreed that I should then work as a liaison missionary for Gethsemane congregation, reaching out into the surrounding Negro community, inviting people to the church, and making membership and all that it implies available to them." The only response to my plan was made by the executive director. He looked at his watch and said, "It's time for me to be going." That was the end of the meeting and of the proposal that had brought us together.

"The President of the Synod Doesn't Agree with You"

On one of the many occasions when I met with the Mission Board of the Northern Illinois District, the theology involved in what we were trying to do was again being discussed. To try to convince me that I was wrong, Dr. Piehler said to me, "But Dr. Behnken, the president of the Missouri Synod, doesn't agree with you." Yes, I knew that he didn't agree with me. The viewpoint of the president of the Synod was no doubt referred to to try to clinch the argument and to prove my position "unorthodox." And therein lies a tale.

Lutheran Church-Missouri Synod church polity is congregational, i.e. under the Word of God and the Lutheran Confessions, the congregation is supposed to be autonomous. A good idea, in keeping with the liberty of which much of the New Testament speaks. If truly followed, the name of God is glorified and the "unity of the Spirit strengthened" (Eph. 4:3).

But in matters racial, congregational polity in Missouri Synod circles has often been abused, ignored, or lost sight of. Indeed, during the past two or three decades the purported autonomy of the congregation has been used to keep Negroes or members of other racial or ethnic minority groups from joining a church or becoming full participants in its life and work, e.g., a congregation taking a vote to decide whether it will or will not accept minority group members. On the other hand, a decision of the Synod, or even the statement made by the Northern Illinois District executive director quoting a synodical president (as though his word had some binding episcopal authority) can bypass the freedom of congregational or individual action. And the result may be a popish legalism.

"Success" in Chicago

In calling me to Chicago, the mission board without a doubt had in mind winning for the kingdom of God via The Lutheran Church-Missouri Synod such Negroes as were "wandering as sheep without a shepherd." There was no controversy between them and me on this point. But despite what we had discussed before I accepted the call, the mission board believed my mission was to be accomplished only by and through establishing "Negro congregations." My concept of the call, as I defined it before and after accepting it, was both to establish new congregations where the geography dictated, and to help prepare already established Lutheran congregations to accept the challenge presented by the racial change that was or would be taking place in their communities. In doing so, I felt a service was being rendered the church beyond a purely mission ministry, a service to the church itself, so greatly needed at the time.

Despite my often bungling efforts among the people in the several communities where I was working with the intent of establishing new Lutheran congregations, and with our "house"—that of the mission board and me—seemingly "divided against itself," progress was being made.

52

People were listening to what this roving, somewhat lonely Lutheran preacher was saying.

The first new undertaking after my arrival in Chicago was in the area near State Street between 91st and 95th Streets. It was called Princeton Park, where, west of State Street a modern middle-class housing project had been developed. East of State Street many of Chicago's Negro elite had their own custom-built residences, some of them costing $50,000 to $100,000. After the groundwork was laid and a small temporary all-purpose chapel erected, the Rev. Moses S. Dickinson was called to take over and to develop the work. At this writing, after about 20 years, this congregation of 1170 baptized members, including 869 communicants, has a church and school building erected at a cost of $265,000.

The second new project was in the Altgeld Gardens community, 130 blocks south of Chicago's Loop. This work was later abandoned, among other reasons because it was discovered belatedly that the people of this community could well be served by a Lutheran congregation not too far distant.

But the chief "success" attributable to my ministry and the cooperation of the district through the mission board was perhaps the development within a few years of what might well have been considered the most difficult mission project of the district, known first as the Ida B. Wells Mission and later as the Lutheran Church of Christ the King. When I left Chicago, it was approaching self-support.

Though the mission board of the district, almost from the beginning of my work in their midst, opposed the theological principles according to which I worked, they were compelled to acknowledge, and gladly did so, the statistical success with which my efforts on the South Side of Chicago were crowned.

At a South Side circuit meeting attended by both laymen and clergy, Dr. Piehler, the executive director of the district, intending to encourage the support of the work I was doing, said, "Schulze knows how to get his Negro members to contribute." If there was an element of truth in what the director said, it was in this that Negro Christians respond to the gospel as other Christians do under similar circumstances.

Pastor Semmann, the mission secretary of the district, preached a mission sermon in Faith Church, Cicero, Illinois, in which he praised the work we were doing on Chicago's South Side. But when encouraging their gifts and prayers in behalf of our work, he added the safeguard he felt essential so as not to challenge them unduly: "I do not say that it is necessary for you to invite Negroes to become members of your own congregation." The Rev. Alfred P. Klausler, who at that time was editor of the *Walther League Messenger* and a member of the church where this incident occurred, called me the next day to tell me what had happened. He and the preacher for the day were invited to the parsonage for dinner. At the dinner table the pastor's daughter, Miss Harriet Fricke, challenged the mission secretary's statement about not inviting Negroes to become members of their congregation. And her father, the Rev. Harry C. Fricke, added that the statement made by the mission secretary contradicted what he, the pastor, had preached to his congregation on the previous Sunday.

With the consent of the Rev. Mr. Klausler, I met with the mission secretary to discuss the incident. What effect the conversation had on him, I am unable to say. I remember, though, that some years later, after I had left Chicago, he told me he had changed his mind in the matter of communicant integration. I hold his memory in high esteem because he tried to remain susceptible to the promptings of the Holy Spirit, even those coming to him through me, one of the least of those through whom the Spirit can work.

"Aren't They Superstitious?"

A real rat race took place between the altar and the pulpit. I would not have noticed it if it hadn't engaged the attention of my congregation made up largely of women and children. Although I learned later through personal experience that this sort of thing happened regularly, to the joy of some of the boys and the fright of the women and girls, it disturbed me more than it did my listeners: it detracted their attention, and, what's more, supposing, because of the surface calm I tried to maintain while preaching, one of the rats would have taken refuge under my cassock? This was my first experience preaching at the Ida B. Wells Mission on the first Sunday in September, 1947. There were more to follow.

It was in this storefront mission in the 3600 block on Cottage Grove Avenue, next to the street car barns, that my predecessors had labored since the beginning of the mission some ten years previous. It was here that a Christian day school was conducted during the week and all other church activities took place. When the landlord threatened to raise the rent from $90 a month to something like $130, that was it. I was instructed to look around for other quarters.

The question of where to conduct the one-room, one-teacher day school was easily solved: I became the morning and afternoon assistant "tour guide," helping the teacher, a member of the congregation, to transport about 20 children each school day via street car to and from Chicago's Chinatown, two and a half miles to the northwest. There in another storefront, rented with the intention of drawing Chinese people to the church, the Ida B. Wells school was continued.

Mr. Sims, the owner of Sims Funeral Parlors, was known to me as a kindly gentlemen who seemed favorably disposed toward what "the Lutherans" were trying to do in and for the community. His establishment was on the same street as our old mission home (the one of rat-race fame), a block or two away. He was willing to allow us to use his parlors for Sunday services, and for a much more reasonable rental fee.

The mission secretary, Pastor Semmann, was invited to look over the place and to give his approval. He liked the place, and Mr. Sims. He asked the undertaker, however, in my presence and to my deep chagrin, "Will it work? Will colored people come to an undertaking establishment for church services? Aren't they superstitious?"

This racial stereotype, drawn deep out of the hopper of many more, seemed not to perturb Mr. Sims, himself a Negro. The deal was made.

Christmas Eve arrived, and with it good business for the undertaker. As we came to the parlors that evening, we found six bodies had been "laid out"; the caskets with their contents lined the walls of the not too large establishment. With permission, they were all moved to an adjoining room. Although this new arrangement gave us more space, some of the caskets were still in full view of many of those who came that evening to worship the Prince of Life Who came that we "might have life and have it more abundantly" (John 10:11).

But was it a racial stereotype to suggest that Negroes might be reluctant to worship in a funeral home because they are superstitious? Although our place of worship that evening was all but filled with worshippers—almost all of them Negroes—it is possible that all but the sturdiest of WASPS, had they been there, would have been hard put to restrain even the last vestiges of superstition that they might have inherited or acquired.

One of my predecessors at the Ida B. Wells Mission was a vicar, Harry N. Huxhold, from Concordia Seminary, St. Louis. He had learned to live with the Sunday morning rat race and had become acquainted with many of the stereotypes used to the detriment of black people, including the one about the "superstitious colored people."

During his vicarage year, having been invited to preach in one of the big churches in the Chicago area, Mr. Huxhold spoke in defense of the people with whom he was working and, in doing so, in defense of the gospel itself. Upon his return to the seminary the next fall for his final year before graduation, he was confronted with a protest that had been lodged against him. Because of the sermon he had preached, his protestors wanted the seminary authorities to keep him from being graduated.

Several years later, after I had assumed "temporary" charge of the Ida B. Wells Mission, I proposed to the mission secretary that the board fulfill its promise to call a pastor to take charge of the mission and, in doing so, to call Pastor Huxhold who at the time was the assistant to the director of the Lutheran Child Welfare Association of Illinois. Pastor Semmann thought it a good idea, recommended it to the board, and the board decided to call him.

It seems to have been the custom of the missionary board to submit the name of anyone to be called by them to the president of the district for his approval. After about two years had passed and I had inquired many times as to the calling of Pastor Huxhold, I was finally told that the call would not be extended; the president of the district, the Rev. A. H. Werfelmann, had delayed in responding, and, when he did, disapproved of extending the call. By means of the grapevine I learned that the district president disapproved because he "didn't want two Schulzes in Chicago."

Veni - Vidi - Vici

The Chicago Medical Center was developing (1953). Then already it was being spoken of as the world's largest. Missouri Synod officials were interested in getting their finger in the pie; they wanted to reach at least those doctors, interns, nurses, and student nurses who were Lutherans, especially those of the Missouri Synod. At that time the Rev. Ralph L. Moellering, a young man of great promise, was student pastor at the University of South Dakota. He was called to take charge of the work at the Chicago Medical Center. After he had accepted the call and had begun his work, he was told by the Rev. Reuben W. Hahn, the chief executive responsible for his being called there, "Stay away from Andrew Schulze." Therein also lies another tale.

A thousand or more acres of land had been purchased by the Medical Center developers, and the houses, stores, and other buildings that had been erected there in earlier days had been razed. In at least one area which bordered on the center, large housing projects had been built. Churches within walking distance of the center were few. There was one Missouri Synod church, First Immanuel, whose property adjoined the Medical Center property. Its school on the church property had been closed a number of years previously, and the ground on which the building stood together with the school had been acquired by the Medical Center authorities.

It was hoped that the work at the center could be carried on, not in isolation from but in connection with that of an established congregation.

Since there was a vacancy in the pastorate of First Immanuel at the time, Pastor Moellering was called to function as pastor of the church as well as minister to Medical Center personnel.

My interest in the goings on at First Immanuel, as I have indicated earlier, antedated my coming to Chicago. I was glad when I was invited to attend a meeting of members of the church council of First Immanuel with officials of the Missouri Synod campus ministry and a representative of the Northern Illinois District Mission Board, when they discussed the plans that finally developed into the calling of Pastor Moellering.

The impression I received then, as well as other circumstances, led me to believe that the challenge to the congregation—and therefore also to the person who would accept the call, i.e., witnessing to the cosmopolitan community around the church—was at least not a major factor in their planning, possibly even no part of it at all. Because of this possibility, I thought it likely that this challenge would not be stressed in the letter accompanying the call to Pastor Moellering. I soon learned that it wasn't even mentioned in the letter.

Those extending the call and I were interested in Pastor Moellering's receiving and accepting it. The goals they had were valid; but mine went a step farther. Because of what I considered my responsibility to the Northern Illinois District and the individual congregations within that district, and because I was a personal friend of Pastor Moellering, I called him by long distance to encourage him to accept the call.

He told me that arrangements had already been made for him to come to Chicago to consult with the church council and others, and that he would come earlier to talk the matter over with me at greater length.

He came, and met with those mentioned.

He saw, not only the Medical Center with its potential for the church serving its personnel, but also the community with its silent cry for the Christian witness.

Christ conquered. Pastor Moellering accepted the call, established the program for reaching Medical Center personnel, and became the instrument of the Holy Spirit in opening the doors of First Immanuel to the people of its cosmopolitan community. First Immanuel, after its first one hundred years, became the first Chicago congregation of the Missouri Synod to accept Negroes as well as other minority group members into its fold.

Even the casual reader of the preceding pages describing my relation with the Mission Board of the Northern Illinois District will have no difficulty in discovering that throughout the seven years of my ministry in Chicago there were many times when we not only did not see eye to eye; at times the tension wrought by our disagreement bordered on the disruption of the work mutually undertaken. There are mitigating circumstances, though, which preclude too harsh a judgment on those criticized.

My stay in Chicago from September 1947 to August 1954 was a time when every segment of American society—the church not the least—was being challenged to reassess its attitude toward the black man in our midst. The circumstances of my professional life from 1924 to 1954 compelled me to rethink my theology pertinent to the race issue and to readjust my approach to the work of the church insofar as the race question was involved. Having done so, I was emotionally prepared and theologically committed to witness to the church which had nurtured and commissioned me to witness to Christ where I was called to do so. The lack of background of experience and theological development of those with whom I was called to work—members of the mission board in particular—did not altogether excuse their slowness in comprehending and living by God's will with regard to the elimination of the color line in the church and its work. Such a circumstance, though, might well call for refraining from undue criticism on the part of others who, like me, must say, "There go I but for the grace of God."

When a theological principle as I saw it was at the moment being applied to a specific problem confronting us, it happened more than once that several members of the Mission Board of the Northern Illinois District would defend the principle and call for its application in practice. There was one member of the board in particular, the Rev. Edgar R. Pflug, who understood and accepted the principle and remained firm in his attitude of applying it to the problem at hand.

The first years of Pastor Pflug's ministry were spent in Buffalo, N.Y. There he was under the tutelage and practical assistance of that staunch defender of the faith, Dr. Henry F. Wind, who was often accused of preaching the "social gospel." But Dr. Wind did more than many other great minds in the church at that time to help those of us with fewer talents to shape up our theology to meet the needs of a fast-changing society.

Under the guidance of Dr. Wind, Pastor Pflug was instrumental in establishing the Church of our Savior of predominantly Negro constituency. This experience in Buffalo stood Pastor Pflug in good stead when later he served for many years as a member of the Northern Illinois District Mission Board, when serving for seven years as pastor of St. Philip's Church in Detroit, another church of predominantly Negro membership, and when he returned to Chicago to become the pastor of

St. Stephen's Church which, after years of closing its eyes to the challenge of a changing community, had begun to receive Negroes into membership.

It is a cause for special thanksgiving, as I conclude this section of my book, to be able to pay tribute to Pastor Pflug who through the most difficult years of my parish ministry, moved by the compassion of Christ for people, always stood, Jonathan-like, at my side.

Chapter Four

Missionary Board of the
Synodical Conference

Maintaining the unity of the Spirit . . .

Eph. 4:4

The years of my Chicago ministry (1947-1954) all but coincided with those of my membership on the Missionary Board of the Evangelical Lutheran Synodical Conference of North America.

The so-called "Negro mission work" in which The Lutheran Church-Missouri Synod was involved was until 1963 carried on by the Synodical Conference; and the Missionary Board of that body was in charge of its mission work. That was no mean task. Especially at the time when I became a member of the board, race was already emerging as a great national issue and the church in the midst of the nation was being put to the test more and more to prove its relevance by putting its theological words—reconciliation, acceptance, love, unity, and fellowship—into action where the action could be seen and the words heard.

I was no neophyte when I was elected to the board in 1946. Other members of the board knew it quite well. Chosen by the workers of the General Conference, the Rev. Clemonce Sabourin of New York City and I represented them on the Synodical Conference Advisory Committee, also known as the Survey Committee, which brought to the 1946 convention of the Synodical Conference the resolution that opened the way for its so-called Negro mission congregations to seek and be received into membership in the districts of the synods.

I was scheduled to preach and lecture in the San Francisco Bay area the Sunday preceding the first meeting of the Missionary Board after I had been elected to membership. I knew it was possible that I would be a little late for the opening session of the two-day Chicago meeting, and wrote to that effect to Dr. Karl Kurth, the executive secretary of the

Synodical Conference Missionary Board, who prepared the agenda. His knowing this in advance made it possible for him, if he so chose, to place those specific items that held a primary interest for me a little later on the agenda.

As I had anticipated, the train was somewhat late, and as a result I arrived about 45 minutes after the beginning of the opening session.

To my amazement I soon learned that the primary item on the agenda in which I might have been able to contribute to the discussion had already been completely disposed of. This agenda item was the report to the Synodical Conference of its Survey Committee. The report had been approved by the conference about six weeks before this meeting, but the implementation of the committee's recommendations referring to mission congregations being received into the districts of the constituent synods had now become the responsibility of the Missionary Board. Since I was elected to the Survey Committee by the workers in the mission field and had worked with the committee for two years, it seemed to me that it would have been ethical, even if the board did not think it helpful, that I should participate in that discussion.

It seems to have been the traditional practice of the board to consider as members of its executive committee those who lived in the closest proximity to St. Louis where the executive secretary had his office at Concordia Publishing House. While the entire membership of the board, called the Plenary Board, met four or five times a year, the executive committee met monthly, or, as occasion warranted, more often. The great majority of the board's work was done by the executive committee.

My election to the board and my living in St. Louis at the time qualified me, according to traditional practice, for membership on the executive committee. The board nevertheless saw fit, in those 45 minutes preceding my arrival at the first meeting that I was to attend, to change its customary procedure. From then on the executive committee was to consist of the president of the board, the secretary, and the treasurer, all of whom lived in St. Louis or its environs, and a board member representing each of the non-Missouri constituent synods of the Synodical Conference.

As the full impact of what had transpired preceding my arrival dawned on me, it seemed clear that a plan had already been initiated to make my membership on the board as ineffectual as possible, if not to intimidate me to the extent that I would out of sheer self-defense draw back into my shell and the board could continue "business as usual."

Shortly after my return to St. Louis, I called on the executive secretary. When I confronted him with what seemed unethical practice in following the agenda so as to exclude me from the discussion of those items affecting me and my work with the board, he denied none of it.

Structure of Synodical Conference
in Relation to its Mission Work

Because of the unique structure of the Synodical Conference—it was a conference of synods and not itself a synod—there were a number of circumstances potentially detrimental to a real understanding of the conference's mission work, its problems, challenges, and prosecution.

There were several small magazines—*The Lutheran Pioneer, Die Missiontaube,* and later *The Missionary Lutheran*—devoted to the mission work of the Synodical Conference; but they were read by a very small number of members of the Missouri Synod. The official periodicals of the Missouri Synod, devoted understandably to the promotion of that work which was per se its own, made only passing reference to the work being done jointly with others who were members with them in the Synodical Conference. As a result of this communication vacuum, Missouri Synod delegates to Synodical Conference conventions came with little preparation for a genuinely enlightened interest in the conference's mission work.

Different from the attendance at district and circuit meetings of the Synod, attendance as a delegate to the Synodical Conference conventions was a once-in-a-lifetime happening. A handful of synodical officials and representatives from the two Missouri Synod seminaries were always present, as well as seminary and synodical officials of the other three constituent bodies.

Because I was president of the General Conference from 1930 to 1946, and because of my personal interest in the mission work of the Synodical Conference, I attended all conventions of the conference from 1930 to 1952. It was my observation that the interest of the officials as well as the seminary representatives who attended these conventions was centered primarily in matters other than the joint mission work being carried on in its name. This was due in part, and I suppose legitimately so, to the very nature and specific purpose of the conference as mentioned previously: to foster "the unity of the Spirit."

Two member synods, the Norwegian and the Wisconsin, kept the conference at its major task as they saw it: in the earliest years of my attendance, they kept alive the "Chinese term" question (the Chinese term for God), then the Boy Scouts, the military chaplaincy, the lodge question, and finally fraternal relations with other Lutheran bodies. The Norwegian and Wisconsin Synod delegates came with their theological guns in good repair and well loaded, with plenty of ammunition to spare;

while the Goliath in their midst, the Missouri Synod, always had to take up the defensive.

The Missouri delegates came to the conference conventions with little or no background on mission policy or practical mission work. And the synodical officials and seminary representatives were often engrossed in the inter-synodical controversies which continued for decades. So there was perhaps no other outcome to be expected: both the mission policy and the joint mission work of the Synodical Conference became all but the exclusive concern of the Missionary Board.

About Double Salary Standards

"The love of money is a source of all kinds of evil" (1 Tim. 6:10, *Good News for Modern Man*), and clergymen, no matter of what racial strain, though sometimes without money, are not necessarily without the love of it. At certain times, though, even clergymen in years now past might well have found ethical grounds to engage in a pulpit "stay-out" to bring certain inequities, especially such as were based on a different skin color, to the attention of those who controlled the salary purse strings.

There was a time in the history of the so-called Negro mission work of the Synodical Conference when the Missionary Board had a double salary scale, one for Negro workers and one for white.

When in 1924 I received my call to enter the service of the Missionary Board, the following announcement accompanied the call:

Board for Colored Missions
Evangelical Lutheran Synodical Conference
of North America

Salary scale for white pastors

	Country	City	
Years 1-4	$ 85	$ 95	per month
" 5-8	$ 93	$100	" "
" 9-12	$100	$108	" "
" 13 ff	$108	$116	" "

Allowance for wife, $15 per month
Allowance for child up to 6 years (incl.) $4 per month
Allowance for child 7 to 16 years (incl.) $8 per month

(signed) C. F. Drewes
Director

Whether or not Negro pastors employed by the Missionary Board at that time received a salary scale for Negro pastors, I am not able to say. One thing must have been evident, though, to any white pastor employed by the Missionary Board, if he had rapport with his fellow pastors of another color working for the same board: many of the Negro pastors felt that unfair discrimination existed. They believed, too, that such alleged discrimination had many evil effects, not only on the Negro pastors and their families, but also on the work they were called to perform. While accepting the validity of St. Paul's assertion, "the love of money is a source of all kinds of evil," black clergymen felt that this alleged salary differentiation kept many sons of black clergymen from preparing for the ministry. What is more, this salary differential was a major reason why our work among Negroes had been discouragingly slow in developing.

At one time in our history there was a crying need for pastors in this specific mission field. At the same time there were almost as many Negro pastors out of office as in; and those who pointed to this fact believed that at least a major cause for their seeking employment in some non-ministerial field was what they considered unfair salary discrimination. This viewpoint was graphically portrayed in a mimeographed brochure of cartoons prepared by the Rev. Clemonce Sabourin, who at that time was in the employ of the Missionary Board—depicted in one of the cartoons as slumbering happily, dreaming pleasant dreams. As far as I know, the brochure was distributed only on one occasion, some time in the early forties, to a committee that had met to discuss some of the basic problems confronting those interested in the mission work of the Synodical Conference. Several of Dr. Sabourin's cartoons are reproduced here with his permission. (pages 65-68)

As late as 1944 in a "Review of Negro Missions of the Synodical Conference," a committee reporting to the conference had this to say: "Your committee finds that the salaries offered the white workers in the Negro Missions compare favorably with the salaries offered in the majority of the subsidized districts of the Missouri and Wisconsin synods. *And the salaries of the Negro workers are, as a whole, in keeping with the salaries offered Negro workers in the South at large.*" (Emphasis added) (Proceedings of the 38th Convention of the Ev. Lutheran Synodical Conference, Cleveland, Ohio, August 1-4, 1944, p. 79).

Missionary Board Confronted

"Pastor Schulze is more sensitive on the race question than the colored man," said the chairman of the Missionary Board, the Rev. Theo. F. Walther, at a meeting in which I asked for a reevaluation of the church's

WHY DOESN'T IT FILL UP?

LOOK UNDER THE TABLE!

65 YEARS' LABOR

THOUSANDS OF

DOLLARS

NEGRO MISSIONS

Race prejudice and unwillingness to talk about it. . . . Curtains for those who do.

THE STUFF THAT DREAMS ARE MADE OF

EACH ACCORDING TO HIS NEEDS

67

IT'S ABOUT TIME TO THROW THE SACRED COW OVERBOARD

attitude toward Negroes. Although I would have to deny categorically the statement in its context, and the impression which it was intended to give, there might have been an element of truth in what was said about me.

After I had become a member of the Missionary Board—as I recall it was possibly about the year 1948 when the cost of living was rising fast and congregations throughout the nation were restudying the financial needs of their salaried staff members—many requests for salary increases were being received by the board from individual pastors in the mission field. The executive secretary, Dr. Karl Kurth, was instructed to make a study of the salaries of the missionaries and to present his recommendations at the next plenary board meeting. (It is probable that the secretary, before making his report at the plenary meeting, had discussed it with the executive committee of the board.) After the presentation of his report was well under way, the executive secretary passed out a mimeographed report of the salaries paid to each person on the list of mission workers.

At first glance the report revealed that there were no two clearly defined salary scales, one for Negro workers and one for white. What distressed me, though, was the arbitrary announcement on the part of the executive secretary that the report should be returned to him immediately after the board members had had occasion to look it over. Because of my "sensitivity," which no doubt had become more intense as a result of many experiences I had as a member of the board, I feared that adequate time would not be allotted to a study of the salaries listed on the report that was to be returned to the safe-keeping of the executive secretary's brief case.

I knew that if the racial element was not involved, there were other members of the board much better equipped than I to make sound recommendations for salary changes. One member of the board, O. A. Dorn, was the manager of Concordia Publishing House which at that time employed and paid salaries to more than 400 employees; another was Charles E. Groerich, the assistant treasurer of The Lutheran Church-Missouri Synod. I felt that the only service I could possibly render at the time was to discover if there was any substance to the rumor that was still alive concerning unfair salary differentiation based on race.

With only a few minutes at my disposal, I knew I could not attempt an evaluation of all salaries on the list. So I made a selection of the salaries of a few persons, white and Negro, whom I knew and with whose ministerial background I was well acquainted. I compared their salaries, taking into consideration such things as location, age, family, acknowledged performance, and length of service. One typical example:

The Rev. William H. Jones, a young white man whom I knew as a seminary student in St. Louis, who had assisted in the work of my parish there, had been in the ministry for several years and was unmarried. He was the pastor of a parish in one of our biggest southern cities. Another pastor, the Rev. Albert Dominick, a Negro, in charge of two parishes in the same city, was married and had one child or more. At the time he was about 40 years old, had been in the mission work of the Synodical Conference more than 15 years, was a good preacher and mission worker, and had almost incredible rapport with the Missionary Board and the executive secretary. But his total salary was about twenty dollars a month less than the total salary of his young, unmarried white colleague.

But the copies of the executive secretary's report were returned to him minutes after they had been distributed, and when asked why they, unlike other reports to the board, had to be returned to him, he responded that any member of the board could come to St. Louis to see the report again should he so choose.

A year or two later, at a meeting in Detroit of what was called the Northern Conference of workers in the employ of the Missionary Board, one of the black pastors, the Rev. Luther H. Robinson, conscious of the presence of two members of the Missionary Board, asked whether the board operated with two salary scales, one for Negro workers and the other for white. My colleague on the board, the Rev. John Daniel, then of Streator, Illinois, assured the inquirer and the conference that no such salary scale existed. I should like to have supported him by the assurance that no discrimination based on race was being practiced by the board. I was not able to do so.

Silence Can Be Lovelessness, if not Hate

In 1955, when I was a guest in the home of a Mennonite, a member of the faculty of Goshen College at Goshen, Indiana, the professor told me that a Mennonite woman missionary, while on furlough in the United States, was asked what she thought of the Africans among whom she was working. She responded, "I love their souls but I hate their bodies." A clearer and more unholy dichotomy between body and soul would be hard to find. The woman was honest, though; no doubt she had expressed the innermost feeling of her own soul.

There are those in the church who would have the gospel preached to "save the souls" of people of an ethnic or racial group different from their own, who nevertheless are bent on doing or saying nothing that would directly tend toward eliminating such elements in society as degrade and dehumanize its victims. They may be able to say at least with some degree of honesty, "we do not hate their bodies." Yet by their silence and inaction—limiting themselves to "saving souls"—such persons have aided and abetted the injustice in society that destroys human personalities and lives.

If there was any specific evil, sin or weakness to be found lying before the door of the Synodical Conference Missionary Board, which the grace of God alone could remove, it was their almost total silence on the subject of racial injustice. Being closer to the mission work of the Synodical Conference and the people to be served through such work than other officials and churchmen in the Synodical Conference, they might well have joined St. Paul in saying, "Who is made to fall and I am not indignant?" (2 Cor. 11:29)

Whether the Missionary Board was present en masse at the Synodical Conference convention in Indianapolis in 1936 when Dr. Behnken quashed the resolution recommending a first feeble step toward the integration of congregations of predominantly Negro constituency, I do not know. However, no matter how many were present, not one of them said a mumbling word to counter the statement of the president.

As late as 1943 the attitude of the Missionary Board of the Synodical Conference on race relations was seemingly little different from that held by people in our society in general. Executive Secretary Louis A. Wisler, in a paper presented at a board meeting in September of that year, stated that all efforts to bring the races together "can only result in the greatest harm and obstruction in . . . the Christian Church," since God separated the races as He separated the languages at the Tower of Babel. Wisler's essay was unanimously accepted by the Missionary Board with a vote of thanks. (Missionary Board minutes, September 8 and 9, 1943.)

"Never the Twain Shall Meet"

What St. Paul wrote concerning the members of the church at Corinth in his day may well be said of the majority of the congregations of Negro constituency within the Synodical Conference, especially in the first half century of its so-called Negro mission work, "Not many of you were wise according to worldly standards, not many were powerful, not many were of noble birth" (1 Cor. 1:26). There were some though. During the second half century of this work there were many more. None of them, however, were at any time members of the Missionary Board which, from a human viewpoint, largely controlled the destiny of this work. The inclusion of one or more Negroes on the board could have been a gesture of good will, but it could have been much more. It could have

71

helped in a very direct way to bring the Synodical Conference, and through it The Lutheran Church-Missouri Synod, out of its outmoded and one-sided approach to the race issue.

(When a Negro, Richard K. Fox, Sr. in the 1950's was appointed to fill a vacancy on the Board for Foreign Missions of the Missouri Synod, this action was hailed with delight by workers on the India mission field.)

The entire blame for the omission of Negroes from membership on the Synodical Conference Missionary Board, often referred to as the *Negro* mission board, cannot be laid at the door of the nominations committees. These committees would no doubt have welcomed recommendations from board members, especially from the executive secretary in charge of this work. Perhaps "without malice aforethought," it happened more than once that friends of board members were elected to become fellow-members; and at least in one instance a relative of the executive secretary through marriage, the Rev. Paul L. Kluender, became a member. The board knew the nature of the work entrusted to it better than the Synodical Conference delegates and those whom the delegates elected to membership on the nominations committee. It is quite possible, though, that at least in many instances the board members could not, with intelligence, have recommended a Negro as a candidate because, in their personal, social and church life, they had little intimate contact with Negroes.

An illustration may be found in the fact that the three executive secretaries, the Rev. C. F. Drewes, the Rev. Louis A. Wisler, and the Rev. Karl Kurth, who had their offices in St. Louis and resided there, lived, each during his incumbency in office, in all-white communities, and were members of congregations of white membership. Had they so chosen, they might well have lived in predominantly Negro communities. They could also have had membership in one of our predominantly Negro congregations, which would have afforded them a rich opportunity to become personally identified with black people.

Tract on Race Issue Published by Board

When the times were calling for change, when everywhere, in church and state, people were becoming aware of the race issue and seeking solutions, and when requests were being received from a number of sources for the Missionary Board to speak out on the subject, the board decided to do something about it.

A tract was to be prepared which would be offered for sale, a statement that could also be used by the executive secretary whenever he was asked to say something about the race issue. It was to be a brief compendium that he and others would have at their fingertips, to be enclosed with a courteous reply to written inquiries.

Following the conservative pattern which had been in vogue in our circles when a moot question called for a confrontation, the Missionary Board asked a member of the faculty of Concordia Seminary in St. Louis, in this instance, Dr. John H. C. Fritz, the dean of students, to write the tract.

The dean was a good man, and competent within the range of his theological and sociological understanding. When I was the pastor of St. Philip's Church in St. Louis, I had on a number of occasions sought his help and advice and was not disappointed. In spite of the esteem in which I held the dean, I thought the board should have sought someone else to write the statement, someone with a background of study and experience in the field of race relations. If the tract were theologically sound and written with insight of the sociological and political problems involved, and if it were in the best sense prophetic, it could have helped the Synodical Conference as well as The Lutheran Church-Missouri Synod, toward a responsible course of action in keeping with what Christ meant when He said, "You are the salt of the earth . . . you are the light of the world" (Matt. 5-13, 14).

After the tract had been written, a copy was sent to each member of the board, to be discussed at the next plenary meeting. The tract included many statements that were good, and in a better context could have served the church well. But when I (a member of the board at that time) began reading it, I discovered that in the final analysis it was to a large extent a defense of the church's past; in some places it was paternalistic and left loopholes for the segregationist to vindicate himself. It was a statement which, if published shortly after World War I, might have reflected a measure of understanding and growth, but not in 1948 and after World War II.

Before leaving for the board meeting, I worked out a strategy which I intended to follow when the tract would be discussed. Knowing pretty well the thinking of the board members on the whole race issue, I felt quite sure that the tract would be adopted, possibly with some minor changes, but with its basic structure left intact. I therefore decided to participate in the discussion, commending what I thought worthy of commendation and criticizing other sections, hoping that if it were adopted at least some of the worst statements would be eliminated; and after the tract was discussed and a motion made to adopt it, I would nevertheless have to vote against it.

When the discussion began, I told my colleagues that I intended to participate fully, but before a vote would be taken I would like to exercise the privilege of making a statement on the tract in its entirety. The discussion was carried over into an evening session, and when at 9:30 no consensus had been reached, I was asked to meet that same night with a member of the board, the Rev. Raymond R. Pollatz, Sr., who had more background in the way of practical experience than the others. The outcome of my meeting with him was intended to be a statement that the two of us would present to the board the next morning which the entire board could then adopt.

The meeting was adjourned, and after the two of us had indulged in a premidnight snack we began working on our assignment. My colleague was at first unusually conciliatory. He was ready to agree to many changes that I proposed; he even undergirded them with some arguments of his own. As the hours wore on though, I found that we were not in agreement as to the basic structure of the proposed tract. And, what is more, I found my defense mechanisms becoming shaky. At about 2 a.m. we decided to quit.

When we reported to the board that morning, most of the changes we had agreed on during the night session were adopted; in every other respect the tract as submitted remained untouched. Before the vote was taken to accept the proposed tract in this form, I told the board why I objected to the tract as such, but that I had sought the change or elimination of certain words or phrases so that in the event of its being accepted for publication, basically in its original form, it would have been at least somewhat improved. I told them that I would, in all good conscience, be compelled to vote against a resolution to adopt the tract because of its content as such and because I felt it would not be acceptable to our workers in the mission field and would be detrimental to the image of the church.

The board voted to accept the tract. It was given the title "The Lutheran Church and the Negro." A small quantity was printed and, after a number of negative responses and reviews, it found its rightful place among those items of historic interest which help to present an honest *picture of our past.*

"Cosmopolitan" Churches—for Negroes!

Milwaukee is a Lutheran stronghold. Within the city there were, at least until the 1950's, many numerically strong Lutheran congregations of all synodical varieties; and not the least among them were the congregations affiliated with the Synodical Conference. In the midst of all these congregations another one was to be established by the Synodical Conference Missionary Board.

The Rev. Gerhard Groerich was commissioned to investigate the possibilities as to where the work should begin, and what measure of success could be anticipated. He reported to the board that some Negro Lutherans had tried to "barge" their way into one of the Missouri Synod churches there. When asked of what racial or ethnic background the people were whom he envisioned being brought into the church that he anticipated being established, he responded: It was to be a cosmopolitan congregation.

What an admission of the sin of omission that Milwaukee congregations were involved in, by passing by the black people in their work of kingdom building. If there were prospects of establishing a "cosmopolitan" Lutheran congregation in a community in walking distance of other Lutheran churches, it must be expected that they themselves were not cosmopolitan; and their cooperating in or even condoning the establishment of a congregation thus described was ipso facto an admission that they were not what the new congregation was to be, "cosmopolitan," that is, Negro-including.

This is how the Milwaukee mission project was interpreted by *The Lutheran Witness:* "In Milwaukee the Wisconsin and the Missouri Synod . . . are sharing the expenses of St. Philip's Mission, Milwaukee's first inter-racial Lutheran Church, designed to serve the large Negro population of the city's Sixth Ward. The mission will 'refuse membership to no one just because he happens to be of a different color.'" (Vol. 72, p. 64, Feb. 17, 1953)

Like Milwaukee, the Twin Cities (St. Paul and Minneapolis) have a very large Lutheran population. Here, as in Milwaukee, the Wisconsin Synod had a comparatively large constituency, and, next to the Missouri Synod, was the largest synodical body holding membership in the Synodical Conference at the time the following event occurred.

In the middle of this century, black people were still somewhat of an oddity in the Twin Cities, especially in Minneapolis. One Missouri Synod congregation, Redeemer in St. Paul, under the pastoral leadership of the Rev. Herbert F. Lindemann, had already made a beginning of receiving Negroes into membership when more and more of them began to move into the community. At the same time, though, some black people had already begun to move into an area in Minneapolis where Lutheran churches were well established, but none of those in the fellowship of the Synodical Conference had begun to extend the welcoming hand to their Negro neighbors. So the Synodical Conference Missionary Board was asked to assist in establishing a congregation in Minneapolis as they had helped to do in Milwaukee. The result was the beginning of another "cosmopolitan" congregation—"for Negroes"; and it too was typically given the name St. Philip's.

The irony of it all is to be seen in the fact that there were a number of Lutheran churches in the general area where the new mission was begun, and within several blocks a large, well-established Wisconsin Synod church.

When the Synodical Conference began its mission work in 1877, it was carried on within the framework of segregation, and the pattern was still very much in evidence in the middle of the 20th century. Tradition stubbornly resists change, especially when public opinion disfavors it. A good theology and Christian stewardship notwithstanding, church officials too may be tempted to stick with the status quo when change runs counter to popular opinion.

To Protest Inside or Outside the Power Structure

Membership on the Missionary Board of the Synodical Conference from 1946 to 1952 might well have been a joyful and exciting experience. Things were beginning to happen in the church in the area of race relations. The predecessor of the National Council of Churches of Christ in the U.S.A. had just issued a statement both challenging and prophetic, to work "for a non-segregated church and a non-segregated society." The Synodical Conference as well as The Lutheran Church-Missouri Synod adhered to a sound biblical doctrine of the atonement through the death and resurrection of Jesus Christ. Because its voice was still being heard and listened to by its constituents, it had a God-given golden opportunity to step into the vanguard, leading its people in the way that Christ would have them go in the years ahead, years of foreboding trouble and challenging opportunity. To have been a member of the board to which the Synodical Conference might well have looked for direction at that time could have been an exciting and joyful experience indeed. The other members of the board were almost without exception persons with whom one might gladly have walked arm in arm in mutual faith and trust. Most of them have since gone to their eternal rest.

My experiences, as I have tried to describe them, will help the reader understand why on more than one occasion during those eventful six years I had the inclination to resign from membership on the Missionary Board. One such occasion (and it was, of course, before the days of the cry for black power): The president of Immanuel Lutheran College at Greensboro, N.C., Dr. Henry Nau, had resigned and the board was discussing calling someone to succeed him. I suggested that, before going into the matter of calling for candidates and then selecting one, the board should have a thorough study made of the advisability of retaining the institution.

There were good reasons why my colleagues on the board might well have taken time to consider the matter. A regular item in the board's report to the Synodical Conference at its biennial conventions—which was usually a matter of some debate on the floor of the convention— was a reconsideration of the status quo of the institution at Greensboro. The primary purpose of the school as conceived by the Synodical Conference was the preparation of Negroes to become pastors and teachers in the so-called Negro missions of the Synodical Conference. But the number of those who were graduated from Immanuel and entered the mission field was lamentably small, and their preparation for the ministry costly and inadequate.

My reason for suggesting a study of the institution was not primarily the economic or stewardship or even the manpower aspect of the problem; it was rather the pattern of segregation that gave me concern. With the office of the president vacant, I reasoned, a more objective study could be made as to whether the school was to be or not to be.

After a few moments' pause, board member Dorn, evidently perturbed by the suggestion I had made, said that he was tired of the race question being injected into so many discussions at board meetings and that his time was too valuable for that. The chairman of the board, as he had on many occasions, went on with other business.

Whether it was at the time of the above-mentioned experience or not, I am not sure. I called on Dr. O. H. Theiss, who was then the executive secretary of the Walther League, whose counsel I had sought on a number of occasions, and related to him the many disheartening experiences I had had as a member of the Synodical Conference Missionary Board. This time I sought his advice as to whether I should remain on the board, or resign and submit my resignation in the form of an open letter to those directly involved, especially the workers in the mission field who were members of the General Conference. To resign in such a forceful manner I thought might well be justified, with the race issue at the point of explosion; and I felt that the members of the board who were or could have been in a position to give guidance to the church were seemingly not willing to take the first step away from the status quo to a more responsible Christian stance and witness. Dr. Theiss advised me to stay on the board in the hope of being more influential inside than outside the power structure. For better or worse, I followed his advice.

My membership on the board expired in 1952. It seems to have been customary that, once on the board, one would be renominated unless one

77

chose not to be a candidate. Since the individual constituent synods of the Synodical Conference, through their elected delegates, nominated their own synodical representatives on the board, a caucus of Missouri Synod delegates was called by its president, Dr. Behnken—at the 1952 Synodical Conference convention—to set up their slate of candidates. When my name was proposed for nomination, someone immediately asked the question, "Can someone who is the pastor of a congregation that is supported by the Synodical Conference through its Missionary Board be a member of that board? "No," was the answer that came back from the chairman.

To understand what was involved, it must be borne in mind that when I became a member of the board in 1946 I was the pastor of a self-supporting congregation; in 1952 I was a missionary-at-large employed by the Northern Illinois District. Although my salary check was issued by the district treasurer, the district was being reimbursed for at least a part of my salary by the Synodical Conference Missionary Board. Though there was no constitutional rule and no precedent to that effect, I was declared ineligible for reelection because of the reimbursement the Northern Illinois District was receiving.

Ironically, the name of the Rev. Erich H. Wildgrube of New Orleans, whose congregation, St. Paul, had been established by the Synodical Conference and had been subsidized by the conference for many decades, was suggested for nomination. (He, incidentally, was known for his non-integration stance.) He was nominated.

After the Missouri Synod caucus was adjourned, the Rev. William Schiebel of Washington, D.C., himself a pastor of a congregation formerly subsidized by the Synodical Conference, showed the president of the Synod the report made to the convention by the Missionary Board which revealed that the New Orleans congregation was still receiving some subsidy. Whereupon the president called another caucus. When he told the delegates that, according to the rule established in my case, the New Orleans pastor was also ineligible for membership on the board, the treasurer of the Synodical Conference rose to tell the chairman that he was in error. The treasurer was then given the evidence that the board's report itself revealed; and the delegates nominated someone else.

"Don't Do Anything about it—It's Coming"

A battle of words had been carried on for six years. Was it after all worthwhile? On one occasion after the Missionary Board had met all day and had reassembled for dinner, Dr. Karl Kurth, the executive secretary, told me privately that he agreed with me in principle and that we differed only in its application. How we differed, though, may be gleaned from the following.

78

The executive secretary had been invited to a small conference of workers in the Synodical Conference mission field. He came. The workers were discussing in broad terms the whole race issue confronting the church. He told them that he had just returned from a trip to the west coast where a congregation wanted to move out of the community where some Orientals and Negroes had moved in. The congregation had offered to sell their church property to the Synodical Conference Missionary Board so that after they had moved the board could continue the work there among the newcomers in the community. When it appeared that the executive secretary was inclined to recommend to his board that they consider the congregation's offer favorably, the workers asked him if he had taken advantage of the opportunity to confront the congregation with the alternative of remaining in the community and doing the work which God had placed before their door. The executive secretary responded to the effect that the time was coming when such things would happen. His policy was expressed in these words, "Don't do anything about it. It's coming." This statement in a sense was an explanation of what he meant when he told me later that he agreed with me in principle but not in its application.

The whole philosophy behind the attitude, not only of the Northern Illinois District of The Lutheran Church-Missouri Synod and the Missionary Board of the Synodical Conference, but also of the power structure of the Missouri Synod in general in not speaking out on the race issue was perhaps expressed very succinctly in the words, "Don't do anything about it. It's coming." This is no harsh judgment. It is rather an attempt at putting "the best construction on everyhing." I am assuming from the context in which the words, "it's coming," were spoken, that the executive secretary was looking with favor toward the day when black people, Orientals, and every other segment of our society now thought of as a minority would be sought for and joyfully welcomed into the full fellowship of the local congregation. In assuming, however, that those in the power structure of the Synodical Conference and The Lutheran Church-Missouri Synod favored the coming of that day, one cannot with good Christian conscience condone their not doing "anything about it." The type of aggressive leadership that the times called for was largely lacking.

What was needed during the first half of this century as a stimulus to the church's leadership and for the awakening of a lethargic church was a grass-roots call and demand for change, not excluding some of the demands later made by some advocates of the black power movement. But this call too was slow in coming.

Chapter Five

Conferences and Conventions

It was 1920. The fire and the smoke of World War I had just about disappeared. The influx of Negroes from the South to our northern cities, which began when the war started, continued at an accelerated pace. At the same time the Ku Klux Klan with its racist ideology had been revived and was now spreading its poisonous tentacles beyond its traditional southern boundaries; with it there came a new outburst of lynchings in the South and race riots in the North.

Marcus Garvey, a black man from the West Indies, was adding fuel to the fires of discontent. In some of our eastern industrial centers, especially in New York City, he was preaching a black power ideology not altogether different from that of the Black Muslims of the 1930's and later, nor that of Stokeley Carmichael, James Forman, and others.

The General Conference—a Grass-roots Response

It may be difficult to establish what influence, if any, Marcus Garvey as well as the racial tensions that followed World War I had on the mission work of the Synodical Conference and especially on its mission workers. It was nevertheless at this time that the General Conference was born. This conference was made up of pastors and teachers active in the mission work of the Synodical Conference.

Certain historic facts previously alluded to must be borne in mind to understand the nature and function of the General Conference: the work of the Synodical Conference among Negroes, almost exclusively in the South, was carried on according to the pattern of racial segregation which developed after the end of the Civil War. Not only was it the policy of the Synodical Conference to establish Negro congregations for Negroes, but *the Negro congregations thus established remained without organic union with the Synodical Conference and its individual constituent synods.* The only contact that the individual congregation had with the Synodical Conference was through its "authorized" representatives, the so-called Negro Mission Board. This work of the Synodical Conference was for all practical purposes a foreign work carried on in

80

the homeland and in many cases within the shadow of churches which held membership in one of the constituent synods of the Synodical Conference, usually the Missouri Synod.

There is little evidence that the racial disturbances in American society were either directly or indirectly causal factors contributing to the organization of the General Conference. The members of our mission congregations, however, could not have been untouched by the grievances to which Marcus Garvey pointed. They, like Negroes everywhere in the United States, were able to feel the heavy hand of oppression resting upon them because of their racial identity. Any white person who has established rapport with black people and moves freely in their circles knows that when they get together they need no artificially or artistically contrived conversation-piece to keep themselves entertained. Race is a never-ending, absorbing topic even when two or three of them get together. It is most unlikely, therefore, that at least the Negroes who participated in organizing the General Conference didn't know what Marcus Garvey was doing or saying. Nevertheless, the race issue as such, even as it affects the church directly, seems not to have been the primary reason that caused the General Conference to come into being; perhaps we can only guess why it was not.

While the work in the mission field of the Synodical Conference was carried on according to the demands of segregation—Negro churches for Negroes—it was *of* them and *for* them but it was not necessarily *by* them. The authority for the conduct of the work was in the hands of the Synodical Conference Missionary Board, all of whose members were Caucasians. Throughout the history of this work, those who directly represented the missionary board on the mission field—the superintendents—were, with one exception, white. And after almost fifty years of mission work, when the General Conference was organized a very large percentage of the pastors in this work were white.

Did the *white* element in the conduct of *Negro* mission work have anything to do with what at the beginning of the General Conference was to be its purpose? Or, to be more specific, did the white personnel of the General Conference influence it, causing it to evade or avoid tackling the race question? It cannot be denied that they played a big part in the work that brought the General Conference into being. While there were already in those early days some whites in the work who were more mature than other whites in their racial thinking, all of them were perhaps without exception products of theological schools which at least at that time were not ready to encourage their students to speak out on what they considered "social" questions, the race issue being one of them.

Even after World War II and some twenty-five years after the General Conference was organized, the Missionary Board of the Synodical Conference (as set forth in the previous chapter) was still very reluctant to address itself to the race issue as such. Some 15 years after the organization of the General Conference, the Rev. G. M. Kramer, superintendent of the Louisiana mission field, revealed the same spirit, as reflected in these words: "You up north agitate race; we here in the South preach the gospel." A white pastor, the Rev. Erich H. Wildgrube, Sr., in charge of one of the Synodical Conference mission congregations, who also participated in organizing the General Conference, said to me (as I wrote in Chapter One), even after World War II, and in opposition to those who were at that time still trying to bring the race question out into the open, "Show me one Bible passage that proves racial segregation to be sinful."

But why didn't the Negroes who participated in organizing the General Conference cause the conference, in which they had a more direct and personal interest than their white counterparts, to be so structured at its very inception as to strike at the Achilles heel, i.e., the race issue itself as it affects the life and work of the church?

As converts to the Lutheran Church, with its emphasis on justification by faith, had our Negro Christians become so otherworldly-minded that they were willing to bear without murmuring the "inconvenience" that came into their lives because they were identified as members of the Negro race? Had they absorbed the attitude prevalent in The Lutheran Church-Missouri Synod of remaining aloof from so-called social questions? Or, was an element of Uncle Tomism—a carry-over from the days of slavery and kept alive by segregation—a factor? Did their pastors and parochial school teachers fear that their working for a real confrontation with the race issue would unfavorably affect their status in the church, and their salary?

There was then, as there is today, a legitimate place for a discussion at church conferences of doctrine, evangelism, and administrative work. Since, however, the church does not live in a vacuum, but in the world, affected by the world and called to affect it, church conferences have the responsibility of specifically relating their agenda to life in the world as they find it at any given time in history. When this is not the case, those looking on may be justified in their judgment of the church expressed in the word "irrelevant."

Whether the General Conference when it was organized in 1920 did or did not concern itself with the race issue, it began to do so not long thereafter. Beginning with its convention in Selma, Alabama, in 1927 and until its demise in 1954, the race issue was its dominant concern.

The Wheels Start Rolling in Selma

"On our way with nothing to stop us," I wrote Margaret. My Model T Ford had served us quite well the first 75 miles of our journey to the meeting of the General Conference at Selma, Alabama, in the summer of 1927. In a sense, what I had written home was true, for suddenly our brakes wouldn't hold. Was the trip a case of "fools rushing in"? It might well have been that, and more. But the angels were with us all the way.

In addition to the brake trouble, we had to contend with four flat tires and three blowouts. Around 2 a.m., on a dusty Alabama road our headlights quit functioning. With nothing to guide us but a flashlight— and the angels—the four of us, Pastor Paul E. Gose of St. Louis, Mr. William E. Fisch, a deacon member of my Springfield congregation, Mr. Elmer Zimmermann, a senior student at Concordia Seminary, Springfield, and I arrived on the campus of Alabama Lutheran Academy and College at 4 a.m. Others who attended the convention probably had similar experiences, for it was a free conference, "free" also from any synodical allowance for travel. Perhaps most, if not all, who attended managed to get there the best way they could without financial assistance from their congregations.

The Selma conference started the wheels rolling. Slowly but surely the gut issue—race—became the focal point of conference discussions. In spite of a weak theological undergirding, the General Conference struggled through the darkness, plodding slowly toward the dawn of the day when color would no longer be a barrier in the church and the church would take its God-given place in the vanguard in society for the elimination of racial injustice and inequity of every description.

The discussions at the Selma conference centered in the relationship of the individual congregations, brought into being by the work of the Synodical Conference, to the Synodical Conference itself. Though these mission congregations were considered by the Synodical Conference and its Missionary Board in full fellowship of faith, such fellowship did not and was not permitted to take on concrete form through membership in a synod of the Synodical Conference.

At this 1927 meeting in Selma a committee was appointed to negotiate with the Synodical Conference Missionary Board with the intent that steps be taken toward eradicating the above-mentioned inconsistency. To that end, the committee was to propose to the Missionary Board that a constitution be drawn up for a separate synodical organization to be made up of the Negro mission congregations. The final purpose, as the General Conference conceived it, was that the proposed new synod be accepted into the Synodical Conference as a constituent member of that body. The primary reason for this proposal, as I recall, and as I envisioned it in 1927, was not to improve financial matters as they affected the work and the workers of the mission churches, nor to improve our outreach potential in the communities in which we were working, although there was much room for both. The chief reason was the establishing of a demonstrable or visible fellowship between the Synodical Conference and the congregations represented by the General Conference.

Soon after the Selma convention, with a proposed constitution in hand, the committee appointed by General Conference met with the Missionary Board. From the beginning the board was not opposed to the idea of the organization of a separate synod as such (would to God they had been, on proper theological grounds). The board was opposed to the fellowship aspect of the proposal, i.e., the organic union of the proposed synodical body with the Synodical Conference.

During the next 17 years, until 1944, many meetings of the committee were held, some with and some without Missionary Board representation. A number of constitutions were drafted and none was accepted either by the General Conference or by the Missionary Board. At each succeeding convention of the General Conference this was the most vital issue discussed.

While this struggle was going on, the matter was brought directly to the attention of the Synodical Conference, when, at its 1936 convention in Indianapolis—as mentioned previously—a floor committee recommended that the two self-supporting congregations of Negro constituency be advised to seek membership in the districts in which they were found, and Dr. Behnken, president of The Lutheran Church-Missouri Synod, quashed it with one short sentence, "Brethren, it will never do."

In 1942, after all hope had been abandoned that the Missionary Board would recommend to the Synodical Conference an organization that would be in full organic union with it, and when the General Conference too had become wiser, it decided to approach the Synodical Conference directly, by-passing the Missionary Board. The General Conference was to propose to the Synodical Conference that the self-supporting congregations in their midst (by this time there were more than two) be advised to seek membership in the districts in which they were found, in keeping with the recommendation made by the Synodical Conference floor committee in 1936. When this step became known to the Missionary Board, a special committee appointed by the board (the Rev. Edwin L. Wilson and the Rev. George W. Wittmer) met with me as the chairman of the General Conference. It was the board's intention to try to persuade me to persuade the General Conference to rescind its resolution.

Since 1927 the Missionary Board had opposed the organic union of the General Conference with the Synodical Conference; it was now ready to concede and to recommend such union. But the General Conference had spoken; and I was not inclined to recommend the board's proposal.

First Forward Step in Fifty Years

When the whole question of a God-pleasing relationship between the Synodical Conference and its congregations of Negro constituency was brought to the attention of the Synodical Conference at its Cleveland convention in 1944, it was resolved that an advisory committee be appointed to look into the matter and to bring its findings and recommendations to the Conference at its next convention in 1946.

A similar committee had been appointed in 1942. This time, though (1944), the president of the Synodical Conference, the Rev. E. Benj. Schlueter, decided to have two members of the committee chosen by the General Conference, and asked me how they should be selected. He accepted my advice—that a letter be sent to all workers in the employ of the Synodical Conference, asking them to vote for and thus to select the persons who were to represent them on the new Advisory Committee. (The Rev. Marmaduke N. Carter, pastor of one of the congregations of Negro constituency, had served as a member of the first Advisory Committee, but he was not selected by the General Conference itself.)

Those chosen by the General Conference workers were the Rev. Clemonce Sabourin of New York City, and I. The Missionary Board had two representatives on the committee. The rest were chosen from the Synodical Conference at large, including Dr. F. C. Streufert, the secretary of missions of The Lutheran Church-Missouri Synod, who acted as the chairman of the committee.

Between 1944 and 1946 a number of meetings of the committee were held. At each successive meeting it became clearer and clearer that the viewpoint held by the two of us who represented the General Conference was quite different from that of at least the other vocal members of the committee.

The Methodist Episcopal Church, split asunder before the Civil War over the question of slavery, tried in 1939 to mend the breach by establishing what was called the Central Jurisdiction. This was an endeavor to placate the Southern church by establishing a bishopric that would be non-geographic in nature. It was to be presided over by a Negro bishop, and its congregations would be those of black membership. By the time the Synodical Conference's Advisory Committee first met in 1944, the strife within the Methodist Episcopal Church over this new pattern of racial segregation was well known. And the General Confer-

85

ence had now learned its lesson not to accept any type of organization that would separate its congregations, on the basis of race, from those who claimed otherwise to be in fellowship with them.

Credit must be given to Pastor Sabourin who, in an eloquent and convincing manner, pointed out to the committee again and again the theological mistake and the probable evil consequences similar to those of the Methodist Episcopal Church if a separate body structured along racial lines were to be effected. But each time the committee met, the polarization of the two viewpoints—one for a separate organization, the other for district integration—increased.

It was now the spring of 1946. The committee had not concluded its work. Months had passed since the committee had met; and its report and recommendations were to be made to the Synodical Conference at its convention in August of that year. I called on Dr. Streufert, reminding him of the committee's uncompleted task and that time was now of the essence. The good man's response was, "Yes, I know; but what can I do? You and Sabourin are holding out for integration, while the rest of the committee wants a separate organization." It was then suggested that another meeting be called and, if the divergent opinions prevailed, that a majority and a minority report be made. The suggestion was accepted and soon thereafter the committee met.

The same deadlock prevailed until lunchtime, when the chairman in evident frustration announced that he was very much inclined to resign. Had the deadlock continued, with the result of a majority and a minority report being presented to the Synodical Conference—judging from past experience—the majority report would have been adopted, and Dr. Streufert very likely knew that the minority report would have been the expression of the will of the General Conference.

"The wind of the Spirit" must have been blowing strong that noon hour. When the committee reconvened, instead of announcing his resignation, the chairman told the committee he was now ready to recommend to the Synodical Conference that its mission congregations be accepted into full membership of the districts in which they were located. Whether the chairman held a private caucus that noon with our friendly opponents on the committee, I do not know. Nevertheless, his recommendation was adopted unanimously.

When the floor committee of the Synodical Conference at its convention in August recommended that the Advisory Committee report be adopted, Dr. Streufert with unique, impassioned oratory pointed out the values of the recommendation, especially its mission potential as he saw it; and the report was all but unanimously adopted. That was in 1946.

Two of the congregations in question have become members of the Wisconsin Synod. At this writing the vast majority, if not all, of the rest of the congregations which were formerly under the control and supervision of the Synodical Conference Missionary Board are members of the geographic districts of the Missouri Synod in which they are found. If some of these congregations have not as yet joined the Missouri Synod, their not having done so is a matter of their own choosing.

In 1946 many of us were painfully aware of the fact that, with the resolution adopted, and even implemented, the race issue would not at all be adequately settled in the Synod. A hopeful first step nonetheless had been taken, and that was worthy of thanksgiving to God.

Church Pronouncements on Race Relations

With the 1946 resolution adopted, the Synodical Conference was nevertheless not ready to throw its full weight behind a program that would uncover and help to eradicate racism completely. The Conference was in many respects isolated from the mainstream of American church life. Yet it was not altogether sealed off from happenings in the other major church denominations. For in the same year that the Federal Council of Churches adopted its historic pronouncement calling for "a non-segregated church and a non-segregated society," the Southeastern District of The Lutheran Church-Missouri Synod asked the Synodical Conference "to establish immediately a Committee on Race Relations, national in scope, to study race relationships." The overture asked further that the committee "encourage the publication of books and other [reading] matter on the subject" and that "study groups and seminars" be organized. (Proceedings of the 39th Convention of the Ev. Lutheran Synodical Conference of North America, 1946, p. 43.)

An evasive, non-committal resolution was adopted by the Conference in response to the overture (Ibid., p. 48). It was nevertheless another break-through. It revealed that within The Lutheran Church-Missouri Synod some people were beginning to talk about race relations; and that was a good omen, especially since the overture was adopted by a district, two-thirds of whose congregations were in traditionally southern communities.

(After 1946 some pertinent overtures were presented to the Synodical Conference. Nothing of real substance resulted from them; the Synodical Conference, as previously stated, was bogged down in doctrinal disputes and moving fast toward its demise, so that the race issue could hardly come to the surface in the deliberations of that body.)

The wind was now shifting in a different direction; from 1946 on, the

Missouri Synod was to be more and more directly confronted with the race issue. With the passing of the resolution by the Synodical Conference which made it possible for Negro mission congregations to become members of the Missouri Synod, and with such congregations becoming members of that body, the race issue could not be overlooked or evaded as it had been in previous years. This fact was clearly and pointedly expressed at the Detroit convention of the Missouri Synod in 1965. A black lay delegate, speaking to a race relations resolution on the convention floor, said, "The Missouri Synod is no longer German [meaning white]. *Brothers, we are here!*"

In 1956, ten years after the Synodical Conference had adopted the Advisory Committee's report recommending the acceptance of congregations of Negro constituency into membership of established synodical districts, the majority of the districts of the Missouri Synod had received these congregations into membership. It didn't happen in every instance without a struggle. My former congregation, St. Philip's in St. Louis, and several other congregations of predominantly Negro membership, with the assistance of some loyal friends, had to fight down segregationist opposition in the Western District before being received into membership.

Overtures on Race Relations, 1956

Mr. Otis E. Finley, Sr., an athletic figure, long-time football coach of Vashon High School and the president of St. Philip's congregation in St. Louis, was one of a number of Negro delegates to the 43rd Regular Convention of The Lutheran Church-Missouri Synod, held in St. Paul, Minn., June 20-29, 1956. As he and other Negro delegates entered the lobby of the convention hall, the experience for them might well have been that of passing through a sort of arch of triumph.

The words of the Missouri Synod president spoken in 1936 and quoted earlier were now to be fulfilled, but with a slightly different meaning: "Give a colored man a little and he will want everything." No less than six overtures on the race issue confronted the 1956 convention. In their totality they covered a large spectrum of the race question, dealing with the necessity of the confession of the sin of racial prejudice and the concomitant need for repentance; the evangelical mandate to accept people into membership of local congregations without racial considerations, and that no new congregations intended to exclude members of another racial group be established; that the term "Negro missions" be employed no longer; that all agencies, institutions, et al, of The Lutheran Church-Missouri Synod make no distinctions based on race in their entrance requirements and employment practices, *and that the church "condition its members to work in the capacity of Christian citizens for the elimination of discrimination based on race or ethnic origin, in the home community, the city, state, and nation."*

The morning of the day before the scheduled close of the convention, the mimeographed program listing the items of business for the day, and distributed among the delegates, presented the floor committee's recommendations re the race relations overtures before the convention.

(The Lutheran Human Relations Association of America, organized in 1953, working on a shoestring budget, could not afford the expense of a booth at the convention. Dr. Henry F. Wind, Executive Secretary of the Missouri Synod's Department of Social Welfare, who was sympathetic to the cause espoused by LHRAA, voluntarily gave the association space in his own booth for a display of LHRAA literature. This little LHRAA corner became the impromptu headquarters for some persons at the convention interested in the fate of the race relations overtures.)

Soon after the floor committee's resolutions were distributed, a number of persons came to the LHRAA booth to evaluate them. Among those who met there were Dr. Wind and Dr. Martin H. Scharlemann, the latter a member of the faculty of Concordia Seminary in St. Louis.

We found there was much in the committee's recommendations to the convention that was good and relevant. There were several emphases which we thought to be needful which the committee did not see fit to include in their recommendations. At an open hearing of the floor committee I had been asked by a member of the committee, Dr. Edgar W. Homrighausen (the president of the Synod's Southern District), if I thought the following items could be omitted: the call to the Synod to confess its sins of racial prejudice and to repent of them; and the directive concerning working toward the elimination of discrimination in society in general.

For strategic reasons, those who met at the LHRAA booth thought it well not to press the matter about confession and repentance, and to concentrate on the other, the directive re discrimination in society in general. These words, previously quoted, culled from one of the overtures, were to be the focal point of our request: "That we acknowledge the responsibility of the church in the area of race relations to condition its members to work in the capacity of Christian citizens for the elimination of discrimination based on race or ethnic origin, in the home community, the city, state, and nation." Knowing the Missouri Synod as he did, Dr. Scharlemann asked me if I could undergird the statement with a pertinent passage of Scripture. The amendment to the floor committee's resolution that we finally agreed upon and which was to be presented on the convention floor read:

> Resolved, that since Christians are constrained to do justice and love mercy, we acknowledge our responsibility as a church to provide guidance for our members to work in the capacity of Christian citizens for the elimination of discrimination wherever it may exist, in the home community, city, state, nation and world.

Several copies of the amendment were handed to interested delegates so that the first one to be given the floor could present it.

When the floor committee's resolution came before the convention, surprisingly enough there seemed to be little or no objection to what the resolution said. Then our amendment was proposed; and the fireworks began. A lay delegate, an attorney from New Orleans, objected to the amendment and specifically to the word "home." Did he see in it an approval and possibly the espousal of interracial marriage? Dr. Behnken, astute chairman that he was, perhaps sensing that the old red herring was being injected into the debate, recommended that the resolution be recommitted to the floor committee for further consideration. That is what happened.

That night at 9 o'clock, when the evening session was about to be concluded, the announcement was made that the floor committee would hold an open hearing at 9:30. The number of persons that came for the hearing was so large (between 150 and 200) that the committee had to move the meeting to a larger room. Yes, the winds were changing for conservative Missouri; the great majority of those in attendance favored the amendment. And the next morning the floor committee recommended the adoption of the amendment as it had been submitted, but omitting the words "the home."

As I sat in the balcony that morning, sufficiently isolated from the voting delegates on the convention floor, my hearing seemed to be unusually good. The resolution was accepted with a resounding "yea." It was followed by a few scattered "nays" which the chairman possibly didn't hear, for the record says that the resolution was adopted unanimously.

Almost all of the race relations overtures that had been presented to the convention, as well as many which came before later conventions, had their origin in my office. I was nevertheless surprised when Mrs. Ernest R. Battles, a Negro lady from Indianapolis who was seated in back of me, touched me on the shoulder and congratulated me when this first historic race relations pronouncement had been adopted by The Lutheran Church-Missouri Synod.

The war was still on and was soon to be intensified; but an important battle had nevertheless been won.

Much Rejoicing Followed

There was much jubilation and handshaking on this last day of the convention on the part of those who favored and worked for the pronouncement. If some were disappointed, it was not evident at the time.

I had attended every convention of the Synodical Conference from 1930 to 1956. With few exceptions, and because little progress was made by the Conference in the area of our present concern, I usually went home depressed and with a sad heart. The return home from St. Paul in 1956 was different. Many of those going home by way of Chicago were on the same train and in the same coach that I was in. Some of them knew the sweat and toil I had put into the whole project, and they were desirous of expressing their joy over what had taken place.

The Rev. Erwin G. Tieman, pastor of a large inner-city church in Milwaukee, with whom I had talked previously, though without avail, about the challenge of integrating his congregation, told me on this happy train ride that he now intended to work for the inclusion of non-Caucasians in the fellowship of his church. And it wasn't long after my return that I received the good news that the Rev. Luther A. Schuessler, pastor of Our Redeemer Church in a changing community in Chicago (though he had until this time taken no step toward the integration of his congregation), was now doing everything humanly possible to win the newcomers of his community for the fellowship of his congregation.

The public, at least the news media, sensed what had happened perhaps more than many of the delegates to the convention and Missouri Synod folk in general. The ongoing doctrinal controversy—which was nothing new at Missouri Synod conventions and for the same reason wasn't necessarily *news*—received some publicity. But the item of business latched onto by many of the nation's big newspapers and magazines was the race relations pronouncement; they highlighted specifically the controversial amendment that was adopted.

It was different with *The Lutheran Witness* though. July, August, and September passed and little or no mention was made of this relevant, historic pronouncement. In October I sent an article to the *Witness* based on the pronouncement on race relations. Using their editorial prerogative, the editorial staff eliminated every reference in the article to the controversial amendment. They were ready to inform their readers of all else, but not that. They wrote me, asking if I would be satisfied if the article were printed as they had revised it. I replied that they might do so, provided they gave me permission to write another article covering the items they had eliminated, or that they would ask some other competent person to do so. The abridged article was published in November.

The Lutheran Witness did not respond to my request; neither did they publish an article, as I suggested, to be written by someone else. Some two years later, having received no response, I wrote an article which was published in LHRAA's *The VANGUARD* in which the history of the race relations pronouncement in question was presented. The article concluded with the following paragraph:

> If concerned people bring something to the attention of a church body at its national convention, and that body, after devoting much of its precious time to the question, adopts as its own a pronouncement in keeping with what is considered necessary, and especially if the resolution moves in the area of a vital need for the faith and life of the Church, can a church paper remain silent?! (Vol. 6, No. 1, p. 4, Jan. 1959)

(Something on this subject did appear in the *Witness* soon after *The VANGUARD* article was published and shortly before the 1959 convention of the Synod.)

An ever-growing number of members of The Lutheran Church-Missouri Synod, especially among the younger pastors, were now determined that the church become vocal in this crucial area of modern life. Beginning in 1956 the race issue has been occupying more and more Missouri Synod convention time: at San Francisco in 1959, Cleveland in 1962, Detroit in 1965, New York City in 1967, Denver in 1969, and Milwaukee in 1971.

Words alone, though, will not "do the trick." They may even defeat their very purpose, e.g., when the mere statement is used by those for whom it is intended as a garment of self-righteousness to hide their inaction. But words are nevertheless important, especially when they are intended to and do chart the way for meaningful action. (On church pronouncements, see *Fire from the Throne*, op. cit., pp. 166-169.)

Chapter Six

My Neighbor of Another Color

In those years in which The Lutheran Church-Missouri Synod met in triennial convention, district conventions were not held. Instead, at least so it was in the Western District, two pastoral conferences were conducted. The Western District at that time included all Missouri Synod congregations in Missouri, Arkansas, Tennessee, and western Kentucky. In the main, Jim Crow with all that it implies was either required by law or imposed by custom in those states.

It was in 1938 that such a conference was held in a small country town about 35 miles from St. Louis. About one hundred were in attendance. Since the St. Louis seminary was in the Western District, three or four members of the seminary faculty were there. I had been asked to present the conference essay; and the topic was the church and the race issue. Although I had preached and lectured on that subject on many occasions and in many places, I considered this assignment the most challenging of all.

It was a three-day conference. I was the only essayist. The rest of the time, as I recall, was devoted to worship and synodical business. About 15 minutes after I had begun my presentation, and when I had come to a convenient place to pause, I asked the chairman if the conference would like for me to stop for questions from the audience. Several questions were asked, and in each case, after giving a brief answer, I suggested that a more thorough answer would be given as the reading of the essay continued. The conference then decided to hear me out, and after that to enter into a discussion of the essay.

After the first session of the conference and until I completed the reading of my essay, I observed that before and after sessions, in the morning, at noon, and in the evening, the subject matter assigned me for presentation was being discussed in private conversations by many of those in attendance. Knowing myself better than my friends know me, I knew their interest was not the result of the profound scholarship of the essayist, but the subject matter itself which until then had received very little if any attention in Missouri Synod circles.

Dr. Theodore Laetsch, a gray-haired theological professor, who had spent many years in the parish ministry and perhaps many more teaching theology, had been sitting in the same place during the entire presentation, immediately in front of the lectern from which I addressed the conference. Since I was well aware of the fact that what I was saying was not a part of the theological thought and teaching of that time, I wondered as I wandered farther and farther into the subject matter what impression was being received by Dr. Laetsch. It wasn't long before I was to find out.

On the morning of the third day I finished my presentation. The chairman invited discussion and questions. The professor was the first to receive the floor. In one terse sentence he gave a vivid picture of what I assume was going on in his mind the whole time that I was addressing the conference: "Not one of the passages [meaning the Scripture passages] that was quoted by the essayist applies." He spoke, and sat down. Those who know where the Missouri Synod stood theologically at that time know the intent of this response. It was meant to be a complete rejection of the essay.

A very lively discussion followed. The pros somewhat outnumbered the cons. This would have been somewhat of a surprise to me had I not been in on some of the between-sessions private discussions.

After 15 or 20 minutes of questions and answers, another member of the St. Louis seminary faculty, Dr. Alfred M. Rehwinkel, who was seated in the rear of the church, arose to say: "Brethren, I believe it is not so much the case that the Scripture passages quoted by the essayist do not apply, as that we have never applied them in this manner." The tall professor stretched out his long arms and added, "This opens up a vast vista of opportunity for the church."

At the close of the Conference the president of the district, the Rev. Richard Th. Kretzschmar, asked me if the content of my essay could be offered the church in printed form. On previous occasions others had made similar suggestions. This conference experience caused me to consider the matter further.

Publication Problems

When I first began giving serious thought to preparing a manuscript on the church and the race issue, i.e., after the conference experience just referred to, I was still in St. Louis as pastor of St. Philip's Church. Because of the rapid growth of the congregation and the unlimited possibilities for expanded work there, I thought long and hard, and seasoned my thinking with some prayer too: Could I afford to take of my time to write for publication? Yet it was evident to me that someone in The Lutheran Church-Missouri Synod should do it.

It was obvious to me that, given an enlightened approach to the race question, the Lutheran Church, especially in the North or in the big cities of border states such as Missouri, had a uniquely golden opportunity for working successfully among Negroes. A prerequisite for such work, though, would, in the first place, be an open-door policy and an open welcome on the part of the church at large for the reception of Negroes into the full fellowship of the local congregation. But such a policy, generally speaking, was not in evidence, not even in the North where millions of Negroes had moved since the beginning of World War I and where millions more were soon to follow.

When the decision was finally made to prepare the manuscript, other obstacles began to present themselves.

Since the manuscript was to be directed primarily to The Lutheran Church-Missouri Synod, I hoped that Concordia Publishing House would accept it for publication. Knowing fairly well where the Synod stood in its thinking at the beginning of the forties, I should not have been surprised when the literature board of the Synod did not see fit to recommend the publication of the manuscript. The secretary of the board wrote me as follows: "Since the subject matter treated in your manuscript is in some circles controversial, we deem it unwise for Concordia Publishing House to publish it. This does not mean that the subject should not be discussed."

Whatever the linguistic or literary merits or demerits of the manuscript might have been, it soon became evident that other publishers would not accept it. Though their responses when returning the manuscript were always courteous, it was clear that the subject matter was considered too controversial for them to handle, or it was thought to be too provincial, i.e., applying to the Missouri Synod and for that reason not having a sufficiently broad reader appeal to make its publication a financially successful venture. There seemed to me finally to be no alternative to publishing the book myself; and that's what happened.

Dollars Needed for Publication

The next hurdle to be overcome was financing the project. After ten years of depression, with one-third of the employable members of my congregation out of work during much of that time, I was in no way capable of financing the printing and publication of the book. Neither were friends or relatives at hand to lend the needed money; relatives who did not understand what the race issue was all about were not approached for a loan; those who understood were themselves still suffering from the aftermath of the depression. One friend who was approached for a loan was the cashier of the bank where my congregation had its checking account. On many occasions when at the bank I would stop to chat with him. He was a member of The Lutheran Church-Missouri Synod, and from all appearances interested in the work of my congregation and the subject matter treated in my manuscript. He was unready to assist through a personal loan or by helping to secure a loan for me from the bank.

Augsburg Publishing House of Minneapolis, Minnesota, agreed to print the book, one-third of the cost to be paid with the acceptance of the printing contract, one-third when the galley sheets were ready, and one-third when the books were ready for shipment. The $1300 needed for the printing and publication of the book, *My Neighbor of Another Color*, was loaned to me by four members of my congregation, none of them in any sense well-to-do, much less affluent.

Chapter on Interracial Marriage Added

Dr. Walter A. Maier, a member of the faculty of Concordia Seminary in St. Louis, editor of the *Walther League Messenger*, founder of the International Lutheran Hour and lifetime Lutheran Hour speaker, and a warm friend of my congregation, was asked to read the manuscript and to give special critical attention to its theological premises. He accepted the responsibility, but, being an unusually busy man, gave the manuscript into the hands of a theologian on his staff. When I called at Dr. Maier's office to pick up the manuscript after the study had been made, the critic's evaluation was written on the envelope in which the manuscript had been enclosed: "We must concede that the argumentation presented herein is correct and biblical. But will it lead to intermarriage?"

If friends, such as a trusted theologian and member of Dr. Maier's staff would negate the whole undertaking by simply raising the question of interracial marriage, what might one anticipate the reaction to be on the part of the great majority of those in the church who were less informed and for whom the book was intended? I had thought the question of interracial marriage irrelevant to the specific purpose of the book. I was wrong; the terse sentence quoted above caused me to add another chapter, one on interracial marriage.

The Book's Reception

It came like a thunderbolt out of the blue.

The book was intended, although not exclusively so, for Caucasian Christians, especially of The Lutheran Church-Missouri Synod, those who by their contributions either directly or indirectly had helped to make the so-called Negro mission work possible. The Missionary Board of the Synodical Conference, however, looked upon the publication of the book as a personal affront; and they were not slow in making their feelings known.

Dr. John Theodore Mueller, a member of the Missionary Board, also a member of the faculty of Concordia Seminary, St. Louis, was delegated by the board to study the book and to present his findings to them. After his study had been made, discussed, and approved, copies were sent to all synodical officials and executives of the constituent synods of the Synodical Conference. A copy of the review was sent to me with a covering note expressing the hope that I would receive it "in the spirit in which it was sent."

A few quotations from Dr. Mueller's review:

The author wrote and published his book without the knowledge and consent of the Missionary Board.

On the basis of campus gossip, the author . . . publicly condemns professors of theology.

The author quotes Dr. Vliet as if he favors intermarriage between whites and Negroes and all other things which the author champions . . . as if one's Christianity did not include Christ, unless intermarriage between whites and Negroes and all other forms of social equality were sanctioned for which the book stands. [It may be well to state here that the reviewer repeatedly referred to interracial marriage as though the author advocated it.]

(The author's) constantly quoting from unchristian, Modernist and fanatic Negro writers . . . is highly unfair to the reader.

The reviewer . . . wishes to call attention . . . to the author's reprehensible playing to the gallery, by which he incites the already prejudiced Negro to yet greater ire.

On page 143 the author closes his book with an atrocious story of a hateful white man's abhorrence of Negroes.

In the interest of his theory, the author . . . twists Scripture.

The omission of certain Scripture passages renders him (the author) an unsafe and even untrue teacher of the subject he has chosen to discuss.

He both perverts the Word of God and omits important divine truths which are in opposition to his views.

The book is not the product of sober and mature thought and its extreme views can be maintained neither from a social nor from a theological point of view.

The reviewer cannot agree with him (the author) on any other point except the one of giving the Negro the pure gospel with all its spiritual blessings.

[The reviewer's racial philosophy, discernible on many pages of his review, is expressed succinctly in these words:] The so-called "poor white trash" in the South, so cordially despised by the Negro, is no doubt worse off than the Negro, for *they have the white man's blood and the white man's ambition,* but not the white man's chance. (Emphasis added)

The result of the widespread, unsolicited free publicity that the book received through the dissemination of the review was a blessing possibly beyond the value of the book's contribution. Orders for the book began pouring in; a second printing became necessary soon thereafter.

Word came through via the grapevine that Dr. Behnken, the president of The Lutheran Church-Missouri Synod, gave his evaluation of the book in two words at a Washington, D.C. pastoral conference: "It's vicious." Through a similar source it was reported that the editor of *The Lutheran Witness,* Dr. Theodore Graebner, who was the essayist at a pastoral conference in North Carolina, was asked why the *Witness* hadn't reviewed or made mention of *My Neighbor of Another Color.* His response was something to this effect: "Because of the evident good intentions of the author, I decided not to do so."

Word came from Memphis, Tennessee, that when the book was reviewed there in a pastoral conference, the remark was made that "Schulze must be colored; otherwise he would not have written as he did," implying, I suppose, that no Caucasian in his right mind could conceivably have written the book. Another deduction that can be made from this remark is that white connotes that which is good and black that which is evil; the author as well as the book were not to be classified as being altogether on the side of the pure "white" angels.

At a pastoral conference in New Orleans, attended by the Synodical Conference mission workers of that area, the Rev. G. M. Kramer, superintendent of the Negro mission field of that district, reviewed *My Neighbor of Another Color*. As reported later, the review was completely negative. "The book will destroy our 'Colored Mission' " and "it breathes the spirit of rebellion" were two of the "complimentary" remarks made by the reviewer. An hour and a half had been alloted for the presentation and response to the review, but the reviewer consumed almost all of the time himself.

After many reports had come to my attention on how the book was faring at pastoral conferences in a number of places throughout the Synod, I decided to do a little research on my own. A cursory study revealed that about fourteen months after the book's publication more than fifty pastoral conferences had reviewed it. And since the persons in attendance at these conferences were nearly all white, I hoped that the message the book conveyed was beginning to reach the spiritual leaders of those for whom it was primarily intended, our Caucasian Christians.

Response not all Negative

Dr. Walter A. Maier told a friend "the book calls for an entirely new approach to mission work."

Dr. Paul M. Bretscher of Concordia Seminary, St. Louis, after reading *My Neighbor of Another Color*, wrote me something to this effect: "The book came as a refreshing breeze. I read it with joy and profit. The next time you are on the campus, please stop by to see me." I did. He advised me to continue my studies and writing in the field of race relations and told me not to be discouraged if the church does not immediately accept what I had written. It had ever been so, he said. He added, "Every major movement that called for a basic change in the institutional church came from without the institution itself." He cited several examples: "The redemption of the world through Christ came from without the institution of Judaism; the Reformation of the church in the 16th century, as well as the Wesley reform movement of the 18th century, came from outside the institutional church itself."

Despite the fact that the book was not meant primarily for Negroes, and the prediction that "it would destroy our Colored Mission," it was welcomed and hailed with few exceptions by our Negro and white pastors serving congregations of predominantly Negro constituency, as well as by their congregations. A number of the pastors had the review of the Missionary Board together with an evaluation of the review mimeographed for further dissemination of the book.

These pastors ordered the book in bulk for sale or distribution among their members and others. A few examples: Clemonce Sabourin, who at that time was in Greensboro, N.C., ordered a total of 78 copies; Paul G. Amt, of Philadelphia, 114; William Schiebel, of Washington, D.C., 115; Paul D. Lehman, of Los Angeles, 50. A total of eighteen pastors who ministered to Negro members sold *My Neighbor of Another Color* to them. According to my records, about 800 copies were sold or distributed in this manner.

Instead of "destroying our Colored Mission," the little book, in spite of its many faults and weaknesses, was a source of renewed hope for many of our Negro Lutherans. One of our most promising black pastors said recently that his uncle, who had been a very consecrated and active leader in the church, was becoming disillusioned with the Lutheran Church because it was avoiding confrontation with the vital race issue. His uncle took new heart after reading *My Neighbor of Another Color* and, incidentally, was influential in his nephew's preparing for the Lutheran ministry.

"I Have Changed My Mind"

After I had received and read the less than favorable review of *My Neighbor of Another Color* prepared by Dr. Mueller for the Synodical Conference Missionary Board, and after I had walked the floor several hours and called a number of my friends to apprise them of the exciting news, I wrote a calm, dispassionate letter to the professor. I told him I had received a copy of his review and would like to call on him to discuss the review and the book. About two weeks later I received his response: He was very busy, and, besides, had nothing to add to what he had written; he would therefore decline meeting with me.

I wrote him again. This time I argued, in the best evangelical manner that I could muster under the circumstances, that since both of us had the welfare of the Kingdom of God as our purpose, I would still like to call on him soon in the interest of a wholesome confrontation which should always be possible between brothers in Christ. His response to my second request, although more conciliatory in tone, was nevertheless negative.

Months passed before I met Dr. Mueller face to face. The occasion was the convention of the Western District of The Lutheran Church-Missouri Synod. As we met in one of the corridors of Concordia Seminary, he told me he wanted to meet and have a talk with me. I responded that I would be glad for the opportunity. In the early fall of that year, 1942, as I was on my way to a lecture hall at the Seminary, where under the auspices of the student mission society I was to address the students, Dr. Mueller was waiting for me outside the lecture hall.

100

(By this time *My Neighbor of Another Color* was no doubt well known among the students. A number of them, especially G. Hans Liebenow, had, upon their own initiative furthered the sale and reading of the book. Although I had routinely addressed the seminarians on the subject treated in my book, the attendance at this meeting was anticipated to be and was much larger than at any previous meeting of this kind.)

Dr. Mueller was most gracious. He asked if he could speak to me privately, briefly, before I addressed the students. When the invitation was gladly accepted, my friend ushered me into a nearby classroom. In substance this is what he said: Pastor Schulze, I have changed my mind; I agree with you and intend to retract my review of your book. Furthermore, I would like to call on you at your convenience, either at your office or home, to discuss the matter. This offer was accepted with the understanding that I would meet with him instead of his meeting with me, the younger serving the elder.

No more than the ink was dry on the pages of the book, there appeared in the December 1941 issue of *The Cresset* a review written by Dr. O. H. Theiss, then executive secretary of the Walther League. The review was laudatory throughout:

> Almost every page of the book demonstrates the careful thought and the conscientious study and research which the author has given over more than two decades to the question of race relations in this country, and especially in the Church, admittedly his chief interest and concern. (p. 48)

> The book is not only well written. It is written bravely and honestly. It attacks a serious problem in the Church and in our country not merely with the weapons of democratic principles but with the resources of divine truth which the author finds in the Bible. It is an important book not merely because it wars against racial prejudice in an era of race hatred, but because it challenges the Church to grasp the opportunity to reflect more fully on its faith in the Savior of all men and in the communion of all saints. (p. 47)

In 1957, some fifteen years after the publication of *My Neighbor of Another Color*, the Rev. G. Hans Liebenow wrote in his B.D. thesis:

> The publication and subsequent discussion of Pastor Schulze's book lit the fuse which caused the fires and explosions on the race issue, some big, some little, to erupt throughout the Missouri Synod wherever the book was read and discussed.

101

From my perspective at this writing it appears to me that there was good reason for writing *My Neighbor of Another Color*. In the main it was a factual presentation of much that needed to be said at the time, and at least some of the laudatory expressions of many friends, some of whom have been quoted, were and are true. Nevertheless, in the year of our Lord 1972 I am embarrassed and chagrined by the book. Why?

The subtitle of the book was "A Treatise on Race Relations in the Church." As I see it now, my development of that theme was not only too restricted, but it reflected an inadequate, perhaps even a wrong, theology of the church, of what it is and of what its functions are. Though the book recognized many of the racial injustices of our society and called upon the church to remove the color bar present in the church itself, it did not in a direct manner see it to be the church's responsibility to lead the way in working toward the elimination of racial injustices outside the fellowship of the church, that is, in society in general. In other words, many of the criticisms of the church as found in the pages of this book are criticisms which may well be made against *My Neighbor of Another Color*. The only redeeming feature, if there is one, is that the book was published in 1941 when the church had hardly begun to realize a problem existed and was much less ready to assume its God-given responsibility to help resolve it.

Chapter Seven

Church Periodicals

Much of what appears in this chapter is based on my own experience, especially as I read the periodicals under discussion when they were published, some of them as early as 1919 when I first became personally involved in the racial controversy. The purpose of this book does not allow for much documentation at this point. Those who may be inclined to question the accuracy of my presentation must undertake the somewhat laborious job of reading through these periodicals themselves. A short-cut toward reaching a similar, somewhat authentic personal opinion is to read the 117 pages devoted to this specific subject by G. Hans Liebenow in his unpublished B.D. thesis, "Attitudes and Policies of the Lutheran Church toward the Negro," on file in the archives of Concordia Historical Institute, St. Louis, Missouri.

Synodical Conference Periodicals

In a previous chapter I wrote of the unwillingness or inability of *The Lutheran Witness* as late as 1956 to witness to the necessity of Christian involvement in social action in the interest of racial justice. I shall have more to say about the *Witness* in this chapter. But first a brief overview of what some periodicals of the Synodical Conference as well as Missouri Synod publications had to say about the race issue in decades now past.

Die Missionstaube, The Lutheran Pioneer, and later *The Missionary Lutheran* were publications of the Synodical Conference into whose lap the beginning and development of mission work among Negroes had fallen. These periodicals stressed two major concerns of the church which, under the blessing of the Holy Spirit, brought much good for time and eternity into the lives of thousands of black people when they, after the end of the Civil War and of the Reconstruction period, were wandering as sheep without a shepherd in a no-man's land called "segregation."

The first of these concerns was the preaching and teaching of the good news found in Jesus Christ as Savior and Friend. Throughout The Lutheran Church-Missouri Synod there are today in all sections of our country the third and fourth generation of black people whose ancestors were led to confess Jesus as their Lord, the Holy Spirit using pioneer Synodical Conference missionaries as His instruments.

Many temporal blessings came into the lives of thousands of black children as they learned, in addition to the "R" of religion, the other three "R's" as well. The parochial school system of the Synodical Conference, with its many schools established especially in Louisiana and later in the Carolinas and Alabama, was developed and maintained primarily though to teach religion. The work of courageous men and women carried on in church and school was properly highlighted by the Synodical Conference mission publications.

Another concern of the Synodical Conference was to help impoverished black people through relief money and clothing. The periodicals above mentioned depicted the physical needs of the poor, with an occasional appeal for assistance; and a laudable, homespun social welfare resulted.

These Synodical Conference periodicals, in keeping with the theology current in the church in those days, did little or nothing to point out the root cause of poverty where our missionaries were working; and that cause in the final analysis was racial discrimination which was built into the structure of our society. The church, for all practical purposes, condoned this evil. For more than 50 years it had hardly said a mumbling word against it. When the presence of racism in our society was already beginning to be challenged, Dr. Frederick Pfotenhauer, the president of the Missouri Synod, restated that erroneous theology in the words, "The real business of the church is to preach the gospel. *It is not the mission of the church to abolish physical misery and to help men to earthly happiness.*" (Emphasis added) (As quoted in *Concordia Theological Monthly,* Vol. 27, p. 613, August 1956.)

In later years, when attitudes within the Missouri Synod began to change and almost all Synodical Conference Negro mission congregations had been absorbed into districts of the Missouri Synod, the aforementioned Synodical Conference publications went out of existence.

Missouri Synod Periodicals Per Se

In *My Neighbor of Another Color,* published in December 1941, I wrote: "A thorough search has been made for something printed within my own denominational circles on race relations in the church. The librarian of Concordia Seminary in St. Louis was consulted in the matter. The search was in vain, excepting for a few very general statements found in commentaries and the like.

"While official church organs have been bold in defending the truth, allowing the sparks to fall where they will, even when the danger of a resultant schism was impending, they have been all but mute on this question." (pp. x-xi.)

Referring to the above quotation, G. Hans Liebenow wrote in his B.D. thesis: "This statement is true, of course, and all one has to do to assure himself of its veracity is to read the official church organs" (of the Missouri Synod). Dr. Liebenow is being quoted several times in this chapter. To the best of my knowledge, he has made the most thoroughgoing study ever done on the subject in question.

So much for the period 1877 (when the Synodical Conference began its mission work among Negroes) until approximately 1941 when the United States became involved in World War II.

Missouri Synod Periodicals 1941 –

By 1941 certain leaders in politics, labor, industry, and sports, as well as in the church were beginning to become more and more conscious of the seriousness of the race issue for all of society.

There were no doubt many phenomena that contributed toward the change that began to take place in the overall editorial policy in the Missouri Synod at that time. Among them were World War II, which helped the Synod to move out of its isolationist German shell and into the mainstream of American culture with all its problems; the Oxford Conference of 1937 with its bold and challenging statement on race; Supreme Court decisions favorable to the black man; perhaps, too, the publication of *My Neighbor of Another Color* which was said by some to have been a hanging out of the dirty linen of the Missouri Synod.

Since it is evident at this writing that God intended to use the Missouri Synod at least for a few more decades as an instrument for the building of His kingdom, perhaps the safest way to describe the change in editorial policy that had its slow beginning about the year 1941 is to say that God's time had come; the Missouri Synod was now to put up, or shut up—maybe shut down.

The *Concordia Theological Monthly,* a publication intended primarily for clergymen, like its German language predecessors, was until this period and in this area of theological concern much like the blind man leading the blind. CTM now began, though in a very cautious manner, to address itself to the issue of race.

It is understandable, though not to be justified, that *The Lutheran Witness* "witnessed" to very little in the field of race relations before 1941. But it too, following its established conservative trend, began at about this time to say something now and then about the race issue, but seldom—if at all—in editorials.

In the main, the Missouri Synod was then and still is a body of middle-class people, conservative not only in doctrine but also socially and politically. And, as I have alluded in several places, its president, Dr. Behnken, was opposed to any change in the status quo in the field of race relations. Putting these two factors together, one can understand why those who had the responsibility for what was published in *The Lutheran Witness* were slow in developing a more racially liberal editorial policy.

What with the pressure of a great change in public opinion in general, and synodical pronouncements including one or more directives for *The Lutheran Witness* to speak out forthrightly on the race issue, the *Witness*, at the beginning of the sixties, had become almost as racially liberal as any of the publications of the major denominations of the country.

By the time the race issue was coming to the fore (in the thirties), *Der Lutheraner*, which until World War I was perhaps the chief popular periodical of the Missouri Synod, had become a minor publication. There is no reason to believe that *Der Lutheraner* was less racially conservative than its English sister-periodical, *The Lutheran Witness*, and the German-speaking theologians who set the tone for the Synod when it was still a German-speaking organization.

Unofficial Periodicals

The *American Lutheran*, which has now been succeeded by the *Lutheran Forum*, was published by the American Lutheran Publicity Bureau, an independent organization that had its membership and area of concern largely within the Missouri Synod. The ALPB was both progressive and at the same time more socially and politically liberal than the Synod itself. This attitude was reflected in the editorial policy of the *American Lutheran*, also as that policy pertained to the race issue. In the late thirties or early forties, when I sent an article on the church and the race issue to the *American Lutheran*, not only was it published, but the editor, the Rev. Adolf F. Meyer, wrote encouraging me to send them more materials for publication; and this I did. Many articles and book reviews written by men like the Rev. Clemonce Sabourin, the pastor of Mount Zion Church in Harlem, as well as sustaining editorials, were presented by the magazine.

Though the Walther League in the thirties had some official ties with the Missouri Synod, it was nevertheless, like the American Lutheran

Publicity Bureau, an independent organization. In 1936 the Walther League began publishing *The Cresset,* "A Review of Literature, the Arts, and Public Affairs." This publication, like the *American Lutheran,* was for its day bold in the challenging way in which it approached the race issue. The masthead of *The Cresset* already in the thirties listed among its staff such stalwarts as O. P. Kretzmann, O. A. Geiseman, A. R. Kretzmann, O. H. Theiss, and Thomas Coates. The advanced thinking of these men in the area of race relations was reflected on many pages of the periodical; and when in later years *The Cresset* was published by the Valparaiso University Press, the same editorial policy was continued. The staff, and especially Professor John Strietelmeier, the managing editor, always kept the issue before *Cresset* readers. The material published by *The Cresset* on the race issue was found predominantly in the magazine's editorials, different from the policy followed by *The Lutheran Witness* at that time.

The *Walther League Messenger,* another publication of the Walther League, was intended for an entirely different reader audience, the young people, including the teen-agers of the church. Under the editorship of Dr. Walter A. Maier the *Messenger* was more cautious in its approach to the race issue. An occasional article was solicited for publication, but as a whole the *Messenger* was less outspoken than both the *American Lutheran* and *The Cresset.*

"A People You Can Love" was an article prepared for publication in the *Walther League Messenger.* It was composed of a number of anecdotes depicting the humanness, the wit, the intelligence, and the devotion to Christ on the part of certain black people, members of my parish. It was thought that the article would appear in the December 1939 issue. When it did not, inquiry was made at the *Messenger* office. The answer given was that the article had been received too late for publication in the American edition and for that reason it was published in the "foreign" edition.

The subtitle supplied by the *Messenger* office was "A pastor gives vignettes of the life of the race he serves for Christ." But there was nothing in the article, as the subtitle also seems to imply, to indicate that it had to be published the month in which it appeared in the "foreign" edition; its message could have been just as effective one, two, or three months later.

The article was intended for consumption by people in the U.S.A. where racial segregation and discrimination were rampant. At best it was naivete on the part of the *Messenger* office to have thought that people in Canada, or in Central and South America, would be edified by something intended to help readers in the United States possibly to be embarrassed by their prejudices and to overcome them. Or was the publication of the article in the "foreign" edition (pp. 200-201) the result of fear on the part of Messenger office personnel that unfavorable repercussions from prejudiced readers would be the result of publishing the article in the "domestic" edition?

The *Lutheran Race Relations Bulletin,* published by the St. Louis Lutheran Society for Better Race Relations from 1945 to 1951, was the only publication within the Lutheran Church until then that was devoted exclusively to a discussion of the church and the race issue.

The Vanguard, published since 1954, has as its specific purpose what its name implies, helping to bring the church into the vanguard in the struggle toward the elimination of racial discrimination. The role that *The Vanguard* has played will be considered briefly when discussing the Lutheran Human Relations Association of America.

The chief criticism that must be directed against the official periodicals of the Synodical Conference and of the Missouri Synod is not primarily in what they said in the earlier decades of our analysis. It is rather to be found in what was not said. These periodicals circumvented, bypassed, or ignored the problem altogether. It was given the silent treatment. The rationalization for doing so, as has been pointed out throughout this book, is a faulty if not false theology from which the Missouri Synod, as well as other denominational church bodies, has not to this day been completely extricated.

In spite of the failure, in many instances, of church periodicals to witness to Christ in the area of social concern, a knowledge of what they have or have not said can contribute in a big way to a helpful understanding of our past.

Chapter Eight

Outside the Structure of Mainline Churches

Member of Mayor's Race Relations Commission

Shortly after the 1943 Detroit race riot, the mayor of St. Louis appointed a "Mayor's Commission on Race Relations" consisting of more than 50 members. Two of them were Lutherans, both members of The Lutheran Church-Missouri Synod. I was one of them. The other (and I have no idea why he was appointed) was an active member of a neighborhood improvement association. Many such organizations were springing up in those days in the big northern and borderline cities; and their chief purpose, though usually not verbalized in plain English, was to keep Negroes from moving into white communities.

The chairman of the commission was a Jewish gentleman, Edwin B. Meissner, president of the St. Louis Car Company. Over a period of several years he devoted, as he said, three-fourths of his time to the commission. There were more Jewish persons, including, as I recall, one or two rabbis, on the commission. Stuart Symington, who soon thereafter became a U.S. Senator, was a commission member and the chairman of a subcommittee of which I was a member. The superintendent of the public schools of St. Louis was on the commission. A goodly number of members of the St. Louis Ethical Society were also commission members. About 30 percent of the commission members were black.

What proved to me to be most enlightening and surprising, if not shocking me out of my Christian wits, was the fact that a large number of commission members made no profession of specifically Christian ethics; and yet they were not only well informed on the race issue but also deeply committed to a drastic change for the better in race relations.

For professional reasons alone, if not to qualify as a shepherd of my flock, I had to be informed on what was going on in our society and in the church with regard to the race issue. And to be true to my calling as a minister of the gospel I had to know and practice the ethics of our faith. Although I was slow in maturing according to these dictates of my calling, I could in all honesty say that I learned my lessons fairly well when I compared myself with so many of my colleagues in the ministry and especially with my white fellow Lutherans in general.

After Albany, the American Civil Liberties Union

The march on the city hall of Albany, Georgia on August 28, 1962, was a demonstration protesting the injustices which the segregation system of that Southern state imposed on its black citizens. (More details concerning this incident later.) The demonstration, in which I took part, was the first one in which a large number of white religious leaders were involved. All the marchers were jailed by Albany's Chief of Police Laurie Pritchett. After two days those who could and wanted to pay the bail money were released.

The Constitution guarantees every citizen a fair, public, and speedy trial. Months passed and only five of those arrested had been summoned to stand trial.

In March 1963 I wrote the mayor and the chief of police, demanding that I be tried. Not long thereafter, four of us stood trial and were informed for the first time that we were indicted for obstructing traffic, disturbing the peace, and disobeying an officer. As we had anticipated, we were found guilty by the court.

Soon after I had returned from the trial to my home in Valparaiso, Indiana, the secretary of the Gary (Indiana) branch of the American Civil Liberties Union called me. Because of my participation in the Albany march and the long delayed and obviously unfair trial, they wanted me to be their honored guest at a luncheon meeting. After the luncheon itself and before the beginning of the afternoon business session, the master of ceremonies introduced me. In a few words he described the Albany protest march, my having been jailed, and the trial. He then asked me to tell the group about my Albany experiences.

I knew the personal make-up of the organization fairly well. There were many in the audience who made no profession of religious faith, and perhaps few, at least among the white people in the group, who professed allegiance to traditional Christianity. There were Jews, Unitarians, Quakers, et al. They knew I was a member of a moderately conservative theological faculty, and I assured them that I was no exceptional member of it. I told them that since they were an intelligent and well-informed group, I would say very little about the protest march and the belated trial, but would say a few words as to why I went to Albany: It was not in spite of my conservative theology, but *because* of it; I went *because* I believed that Jesus Christ is God incarnate in the flesh of man; *because* I believed that He died and rose again; *because* I believed that through faith He had given me a new life which was my privilege to live out to the glory of God and in the interest of my fellowman, especially those against whom our white society had practiced inhumane injustice for centuries. When I had finished there was sustained, resounding, and rapturous applause.

A case might well be made at this point for the evangelistic value of a witness made to the Lord Jesus Christ when this type of people knew that the one making the witness had a deep commitment to the cause of racial justice. I have no reason to believe, though, that at their first opportunity many of them became members of the closest Missouri Synod Lutheran Church. All I really want to say in this roundabout way is that those who make no profession of traditionally orthodox Christianity are often more sensitive to racial injustice and more conscious of the demands of even-handed justice, such as that to which the prophets of the Old Testament attest, than many Christians and active church members.

Through the news media my participation in the Albany protest became well known. A Lutheran pastor in Alabama, William G. Kennell, condemned what I had done in no uncertain terms, accusing me of "praying with Jews." The Rev. Edward W. Homrighausen, the president of the Southern District of The Lutheran Church-Missouri Synod, issued a statement to the press to the effect that we had come from the North and were uninformed agitators. When I wrote him in the matter, he responded that he did not know when issuing his statement that I was involved, but had he known it he would have made the statement nevertheless. A church woman in Minnesota wrote that I was unfit to teach religion to young people of the church. A member of the administrative staff of one of the Missouri Synod's preparatory schools wrote me that participation in the march was an "asinine act."

Shortly after my return from Albany, I went on a lecture tour which took me all the way to the west coast. In most places where I spoke, if my speaking engagement had been publicized, Jews, Unitarians and others not professing adherence to traditional Christianity were present and expressed agreement with and warm acceptance of the social action involved in my participation in the march.

All of this happened in 1962 and 1963. By this time many of the clergy, especially the younger ones, had discarded the theology of inactivity. But the rank and file of the laymen of the church had for generation upon generation been fed that kind of doctrine which for all practical purposes developed in them a type of conservatism that made social action, especially in the area of civil rights, suspect at best.

111

The laymen by and large were not ready to change their minds at the waving of a magic wand—either of a "new" theology of social action, or denominational pronouncements of Christian social concern. As a whole, they were not inclined suddenly to involve themselves in social action which condemned their past social apathy and inactivity. It is conceivable that such involvement would necessitate their taking upon themselves the cross of Christ which could lead to being rejected by their white neighbors, the loss of job or business, of family and friends, and of almost every material good this side of eternity. It is a marvel of the living reality of the goodness of God in Jesus Christ that many of them will have made it to heaven, not by the skin of their teeth, but by His immeasurable grace. They will be there together with many of us who in ignorance led them away from cross-bearing for their neighbor, thinking that in doing so we were doing the will of God and honoring Him.

Meeting with Unitarians and Universalists

An invitation was received and accepted to attend and take part in a National Workshop for Religious Liberals in Washington, D.C., in March 1966 under the auspices of several commissions of the Unitarian-Universalist Association. As a symbol of my being identified with traditional Christianity as well as a desire not to march under false colors, I wore a clergy collar during the three days of the workshop. My fellow participants seemingly, at least at the beginning, paid little if any attention to my garb and what it apparently implied. Nevertheless a most sobering experience awaited me.

As I moved about among the group and engaged in personal conversation with many of them, I found that not all who were outwardly identified with the Unitarian-Universalist Church had, at least in their own opinion, abandoned their churches of traditional Christianity in which they had been brought up. They had nevertheless associated themselves with the Unitarians and Universalists because this group had, according to their viewpoint, made their religion relevant to the world of today and specifically to the civil rights issue, while the mainline churches in which they had been reared were still very slow in applying their teachings to these issues. I should not have been surprised, although I was, when I found that more than one of them had been brought up in the Lutheran Church.

About 125 persons from all sections of the country except the far West attended the workshop; about 45 per cent of them were women. A high level of intelligence and a wide knowledge in many areas of civic responsibility were evident, bearing out the statement by Bernard Iddings Bell, in *The Church in Disrepute*, that many intellectuals looking for guidance in the area of social ethics have turned in disillusionment from the church.

National Conference on Religion and Race

President Nixon feigned ignoring the presence and the impact of the war moratorium march on the Capitol in the fall of 1969, while President John F. Kennedy had seemingly welcomed a similar march in the interest of civil rights in August 1962. After the march, President Kennedy invited to the White House many of the civil rights leaders who had organized and participated in the march. He was then already and later in many other ways trying to build up support throughout the nation for the civil rights legislation which he was to propose to the Congress in June 1963. In January of that year he encouraged and gave moral support to the National Conference on Religion and Race which convened in Chicago.

Those churches that cannot be classified as traditionally Christian, and especially Jewish organizations, were not only well represented; they also played an active and important role in shaping and directing the Conference. Of the 67 religiously-oriented groups that took part, 18 were Jewish. Jews were among the main speakers; they were members of important panels; they were on practically all committees. The chairman of the work group to which I was assigned was Jewish. Jews were also active members of the interreligious committee which worked months in advance to prepare "A Declaration of Conscience" which was to be presented to the Conference for its consideration and final adoption.

Several days before the Conference convened a copy of this declaration was sent me. It was, as I might well have anticipated, theologically oriented, but its theology was bereft of any specifically Christological content. In a religiously pluralistic society, however, any theological statement that exalts Christ as Lord and Savior can be accepted only by those who accept Him as such. On the other hand, the elimination of all Christology must of necessity violate the conscience of those who take the New Testament seriously.

I anticipated this dilemma before the proposed Declaration of Conscience came into my hands. In my opinion, however, there is a way in which religious groups of many and diverse persuasions can speak and work together in the interest of society in general, and in the area of civil rights in particular. Such cooperation cannot in honesty be achieved on a theological basis. It can be achieved, however, on the basis of ethical humanitarianism. We observe that type of cooperation, e.g., in state legislatures and in the halls of Congress between persons

113

of good will of many religious persuasions as well as some of no formal religious belief whatever.

The chairman of the important Declaration of Conscience Committee was Monsignor Daniel M. Cantwell, a man whose Christology I understood, admired, and largely approved. The first morning of the Conference I met him in one of the corridors of the hotel where the Conference was held. When I told him of my misgivings regarding the declaration, he invited me to his room to discuss the matter. The session lasted about an hour. He listened to my argument with evident deep concern, and it seemed that what I had to say touched his theological conscience at its very depths. He told me that Dr. Kyle Haselden (whom I knew quite well as the author of *The Racial Problem in Christian Perspective*, and editor of *The Christian Century*) had expressed a concern similar to mine in the first sessions of the drafting committee. A final meeting of the committee was to be held the next morning. I was invited to attend and to present my views. The outcome, however, was nothing startling; the committee made several minor changes in the wording of the statement and that was all.

The Jews and those of the non-traditional churches "carried the ball" at this Conference. They are to be commended for having done so. The Conference no doubt encouraged President Kennedy, who was represented at the Conference by his brother-in-law Sargent Shriver, in his endeavor to gain the approval of the civil rights legislation by the Congress. And the Conference probably helped in a material way toward the enactment of the most comprehensive civil rights legislation in a century.

A further result of the 1963 National Conference on Religion and Race was the organization of regional conferences with similar aims, in Pittsburgh, Milwaukee, Kansas City, Kansas, and other places of racial tension.

The non-mainline, non-traditional churches and especially many Jewish organizations—all of them together a very small part of the U.S. religious population—must be praised for the very large part they played in influencing the body politic to move more rapidly toward the elimination of racial and ethnic injustice and inequity. On the other hand, those mainline churches which still retain a basic Christological theology have a potential beyond imagination for effective reform in society that will make such reform possible in this age of world-wide revolutionary change.

Why, then, have mainline church bodies like The Lutheran Church-Missouri Synod been apparently anemic, inert, and largely thought of as irrelevant when confronted with the opportunity to lead society toward rapid and absolutely necessary change? An answer to this question with respect to the church in the early forties may be found in a news item in *The Lutheran Witness* (62, No. 16, pp. 262-3, Aug. 3, 1943): "Speaking of the race problem in our country, the Rev. L. A. Wisler, executive secretary of the Mission Board of the Synodical Conference of North America declared that *'the race question is not a problem for the church to solve. The duty of the Christian Church is to preach salvation through Jesus Christ and not to deal with race questions.'* (Emphasis added) He also remarked that mission work in Africa is not handicapped by the problems which prevail in the United States. In this country we still have to overcome the opposition of the colored race against the white race, and we still must win the confidence of the Negro."

District Convention Sandwiched Between Two Race Riots

An illustration showing how The Lutheran Church-Missouri Synod was still dragging its feet in 1967 may be found in the attitude evident at a district convention.

In the summer of that year, and not too long after the terrifying riot in Watts, the convention of the Indiana District of The Lutheran Church-Missouri Synod happened to be sandwiched between a riot in the Hough area of Cleveland and another in one of the big Chicago black ghettos. The convention was held on the campus of Concordia Senior College in Fort Wayne (about halfway between Chicago and Cleveland).

In the opening service the president of the Synod, Dr. Oliver R. Harms, preached. The main thrust of his sermon was the responsibility of the church "to get the Word out." The president of the district in his report placed emphasis on the same thought. Then the convention essayist, the Rev. Oswald A. Waech, speaking on evangelism, had as his chief emphasis the necessity of getting *people* "to get the Word out." When the chairman of the district's Evangelism Committee made his report to the convention, his emphasis was the same. He used an illustration: "A woman went into a telephone booth and wrote on the wall, 'God don't care.' What we must *tell* that woman," said the speaker, "is 'God loves you.'"

When no one else seemed ready to challenge what the evangelism committee chairman said, I called the attention of the convention to the build-up for "getting the Word out" by the president of the Synod, the president of the district, the convention essayist, and finally by the evangelism committee chairman. Assuring them of my biblical orthodoxy, I said I hoped no one on the convention floor would question the validity of "getting the Word out." But to assume that speaking words only was the measure of the church's responsibility, I told the convention, was a serious mistake. I reminded the convention that the Epistle Les-

115

son of the previous Sunday, on which hundreds of pastors throughout the land probably had preached, contained these challenging words, *"Little children, let us not love in word or speech but in deed and in truth"* (1 John 3:18). I reminded the convention further that, according to Christ's description of the final judgment, He will not say a word about "getting the Word out," but He will say, "I was hungry and you gave me food, I was thirsty and you gave me drink. I was a stranger and you welcomed me, I was naked and you clothed me, I was sick and you visited me, I was in prison and you came to me. . . . As you did it to the least of these my brethren you did it to me" (Matt. 25:35-38, 40).

As to the woman in the telephone booth, I said, she might have been living in a black ghetto of one of our big cities like Cleveland or Chicago, in utter despair because of the many frustrating problems hemming her in on all sides. She might well have answered, if someone had told her, "God loves you," and then walked away: "You may go to h—— with your god; he's dead."

After a few moments of silence, and when no one responded, the convention proceeded with its well-ordered agenda. The next day, though, the chairman of the evangelism committee met me on the campus and said he wanted to assure me that what I had said the previous day was his theology.

"Symptoms of an Alienation from the Holy Spirit"

Yes, why was the church in 1943, and in 1967, still seemingly inert, anemic, and irrelevant? In a letter addressed to me on July 26, 1943, Dr. Richard R. Caemmerer analysized the problem as follows: "I feel that the race problem, together with a number of other phenomena in our life as a church, are symptoms of an underlying and inclusive alienation from the Holy Spirit." If this statement is—as I assume it to be—a realistic response to the problem of race confronting the church, then a return to an acceptance of the Holy Spirit and His power must point the church toward the way out of the dilemma in which it is found.

As we look again at the church in its relation to the race issue, the words of Christ seem to be apropos: "The sons of this world are wiser in their own generation than the sons of light" (Luke 16:8). And if His words, "I came that they may have life, and have it abundantly" (John 10:10) apply to all, also to those in our midst who are denied life "abundantly" by a cruel racist society; if the church is the body of Christ through which this abundant life is to be brought to people; if, as we say in the Nicene Creed, the Holy Spirit is now, after Christ's ascension, "the Lord and Giver of life," then the blessing of "the Spirit of wisdom and strength," bestowed on the confirmands by the laying on of hands, must be sought through prayer and supplication by those who claim to be "the sons [and daughters] of light."

Chapter Nine

O. P., Valparaiso University, and LHRAA

In 1925, when Valparaiso University in Valparaiso, Indiana, was almost bankrupt, the University was purchased—with much imagination, great faith, and little money—by The Lutheran University Association. Soon the depression years came on, and professors out of sheer love and with the vision of what was still hopefully to come, spent what time they could outside the classroom hours shaking the synodical bushes for the few dollars they were able to pick up for the payment of their salaries and other university expenses.

O.P. and Valparaiso University

In 1940, Dr. Otto Paul Kretzmann was inaugurated president of Valparaiso University. To accept the headship of a well-established and prospering university would have been no mean task for a young man still in his thirties. Valparaiso University, however, was not in that category.

When Dr. Kretzmann took office, the depression had ended, but the winds of war that had driven the depression out of the land—that is, most of it—were becoming more ominous day by day, forecasting the drafting of hundreds of thousands of prospective male students into the armed forces; and without students there can be no university. Another storm was brewing at the time—the race issue; and, as it has become increasingly evident since the 1960's, universities are, of all institutions, the place where the race issue cannot be submerged for long. To understand, however, what the peculiar racial conditions were at Valparaiso when Dr. Kretzmann took office, it is necessary to review briefly the preceding years of the University's history, especially since 1925.

When Dr. W. H. T. Dau became the first president of the University after it was under Lutheran auspices, I wrote him suggesting that he would use his good office to the end that a racially open-door policy be maintained or established. The president responded that no other policy could be justified by a Christian university. Some months later, though, he wrote me again, saying that while the University's policy would be in keeping with what he had previously written, he had since learned that certain circumstances prevailed which would make it impossible for Negro students to live and study at the University. To understand Dr. Dau's misgivings, a number of historic facts must be taken into account.

In the second decade of this century, the Ku Klux Klan had been revived in the land; and the state of Indiana had become one of the Klan's strongholds. The KKK had virtual control of the political power structure of the state and was very strong in northwestern Indiana, including Valparaiso. The racial policy of the school at the time of its founding is described as follows: "The only restrictions that were made by the school in the way of entrance requirements were that the student must be at least sixteen years old *and not a Negro.*" (Emphasis added) (*Valparaiso's First Century*, by John Strietelmeier, published by the University, 1959, p. 33.) The same source informs us that the University in 1923 came very close to becoming a Klan school, for officials of the University and state officials of the Klan had reached agreement on terms of the sale of the institution to the Klan. But the deal was never consummated. Adding to this the fact that a Klan-like psychology prevailed in the Valparaiso community and about 80 percent of both faculty and student body was from the South when the University was purchased by The Lutheran University Association, one can understand why Dr. Dau wrote as he did in his second letter.

I had correspondence in the matter also with Dr. Oscar Carl Kreinheder, the successor to Dr. Dau. Having been urged to do so, the Rev. Louis A. Wisler, then executive secretary of the Missionary Board of the Lutheran Synodical Conference, also wrote the University asking for the implementation of an open-door policy. But years passed, and nothing happened. The city of Valparaiso as well as the University were in 1940 seemingly as far removed from accepting black students as they were in 1925. No steps had been taken by that time either by the city or the University to change things.

The first ray of hope came soon after Dr. Kretzmann became president. I wrote him, describing the steps that had been taken since the University was purchased by The Lutheran University Association, to establish and to implement a racially open-door policy. I encouraged him to work toward pursuing such a policy. Soon thereafter, the Northern Conference, a branch of the General Conference, wrote Dr. Kretzmann, making a similar appeal.

Within a few weeks after I had written President Kretzmann, I received a letter from him which represented the first hope that something

119

constructive was going to be done to change the status quo at the University and in the town as well. He wrote, "I shall do everything in my power to see that they [Negro Lutherans] will be able to come and be thoroughly happy here. That may take time, but *that is one of my opportunities.*" (Emphasis added) It wasn't long thereafter, when the enrollment of Negroes in private schools was still somewhat exceptional, that Valparaiso University began enrolling them.

But before we move forward in developing the subject matter of this chapter, we must backtrack a bit to put it in historic perspective.

In 1943, about three years after Dr. Kretzmann became the president of Valparaiso University, the St. Louis Lutheran Society for Better Race Relations was organized. The membership was composed of a number of pastors, one theological professor, lay men and women, and a few seminarians. Negroes and whites were members, many of whom were active for years to come in promoting better race relations.

Among the functions of the society were the publication of the *Lutheran Race Relations Bulletin* and conducting race relations institutes.

The *Bulletin,* published from 1945 to 1951, was a humble, four-page, inexpensive paper (subscription price 50 cents a year). It was an inadequate attempt to treat the subject of race relations from a Christian perspective. The society had no money and no collateral. To a great extent it lacked also the professional personnel to do a good job. Nevertheless, for a period of five years it spoke out simply and forcefully on many aspects of the race issue, which official publications of the church were still reluctant, unwilling, or forbidden to do. In spite of its anticipated inadequacies, the announcement of its publication was hailed with joy by many within the church. Among the progressively-minded people in the church who welcomed this new venture and wrote us to that effect were: H. W. Bartels, A. H. Bringewatt, Oscar E. Feucht, Elmer E. Foelber, O. A. Geiseman, E. Buckley Glabe, Werner Kuntz, Herbert Lindemann, E. H. Meinzen, Adolf Meyer. Arthur Carl Piepkorn, Rudolph S. Ressmeyer, Osborn T. Smallwood, Wilbur J. Twitty, Leslie F. Weber, and Henry F. Wind.

Under the auspices of the St. Louis society, the first Lutheran Race Relations Institute was held in the summer of 1946. At that time, the Rev. Paul W. Streufert, who in 1956 became a vice-president of The Lutheran Church-Missouri Synod, was the pastor of St. Matthew Church in St. Louis. Through his cooperation and support, this historic institute was conducted at St. Matthew, located in a suburban community. Pastor Streufert received a number of threatening phone calls because of the institute, but nothing untoward happened.

The institute, which had its beginning on Friday evening and ended on Sunday afternoon, attracted a total of 1300 people. Among those in attendance was a goodly number of Negroes; and that, to say the least, was an unusual phenomenon for that time, in that place. An embryonic Lutheran ecumenicity was also involved: the Rev. Ervin E. Krebs, the executive secretary of Negro mission work of the American Lutheran Church, was invited and attended this institute structured within the Missouri Synod.

Two outstanding persons were on the program: Dr. Henry Nau, the president of Immanuel College in North Carolina, and the Rev. Clemonce Sabourin of Mt. Zion Church in Harlem on Manhattan Island in New York City. Foreshadowing much of what Pastor Sabourin was to say and write in later years was the sermonic lecture he delivered at the institute, later printed and disseminated: "While the Devil Dances."

The 1946 institute was the precursor of many that were to follow. In 1947 another institute was held in St. Louis under the same auspices. The third and fourth institutes were held in Chicago, in 1948 and 1949. At the time of the 1948 institute there was no Chicago-based organization to sponsor it. An ad hoc committee of concerned people of greater Chicago, with the assistance of the St. Louis Society for Better Race Relations, structured and executed the institute program.

At one of the Chicago institutes something happened that was not a part of the program but nevertheless served the several purposes of the institute in a forceful and dramatic way.

An evening banquet was scheduled at a hotel near First St. Paul Church where the institute was being conducted. Shortly before the guests were to arrive at the hotel, I went there to check certain details. To my amazement I found that the desk clerk, after learning that I was connected with the institute, did everything possible in a subtle manner to demonstrate that the hotel was not too happy to serve our interracial group. After trying without avail to secure certain information relative to the scheduled banquet, I asked to see the hotel manager. I was told rather bluntly that he was not in. I asked to see someone who could speak for the manager but received a similar response. Finally, in desperation, I found my own way to the dining room where approximately 200 guests were to be served.

In the dining room there were four or five card tables on which dishes and flatware had been stacked. Along one of the walls two or three dozen folding chairs had been piled up. An old, crudely-painted piano graced one corner of the room. That was all.

121

Soon several Negro waiters began to bring in the food in large bowls, and the coffee in a big urn; all was placed on the card tables. I asked one of the waiters if I could speak to the manager or the headwaiter. The response was evasive, but the facial expression of the waiter revealed empathy and understanding. Then the guests arrived, Lutherans from several states, Negroes and Caucasians, clergy and laity.

The next day the Rev. Alfred P. Klausler, editor of the *Walther League Messenger*, and I, after a brief meeting at Walther League headquarters about two blocks from the hotel, went there to discuss with the manager what happened the night before. He was apologetic: the head waiter had no doubt misunderstood what was to be done; the manager would call him into the office for an explanation. But we understood without the waiter being called in. We concluded that the waiter would have had but one alternative: He would have tried to camouflage what really happened, or spoken the truth and suffered the loss of his job.

When Pastor Klausler arranged for the banquet, he probably did not mention the interracial character of our group. When some appeared at the hotel to register for housing, the management, realizing that their Jim Crow pattern was being threatened, tried in every subtle manner to discourage something of the same nature happening again.

This otherwise unfortunate incident brought into clear focus the problem of racial discrimination, well understood by our Negro guests, but seldom if ever experienced by our white friends. It was a fellowship across racial lines in the suffering borne by Negroes for many generations. It was, at least for our white guests, a lesson that sermons and institute lectures, all good in themselves, could never teach.

LHRAA Comes into Being

Dr. Kretzmann had little if anything to do with the origin and development of Lutheran race relations institutes until 1949. From that time on, though, due to his interest and influence, the institutes changed, and with them the trend in race relations in The Lutheran Church-Missouri Synod. Valparaiso University became the home of the institutes that were to follow, as well as the geographic center of a vigorous approach in the Missouri Synod to the problem of race.

Shortly after the 1949 institute, the Rev. Herbert Knopp, Coordinator of University Relations, brought the invitation of Dr. Kretzmann—to those who until then had spearheaded the movement—to bring the institute onto the campus of Valparaiso University. And that's what happened. Under the co-sponsorship of the two Lutheran societies for better race relations (one in St. Louis and the other in Chicago) and with the cooperation of the University—i.e., the cooperation of Dr. Kretzmann—

122

the first annual Valparaiso University Institute on Human Relations was held on the campus in the summer of 1950.

By the time of the 1953 institute, sufficient interest had been awakened to encourage a further step. Institute promoters now wanted to broaden their activity from a once-in-a-year happening to a work that would be carried on cooperatively throughout the year. They wanted the good ideas set forth at the institutes to influence the church on all levels beyond that of the individual witness back home on the part of those who attended the institutes. It was decided to form an association of Lutherans who wanted to assist the church in coming to grips with the race issue with all the potential at the church's disposal. With this decision made, the Lutheran Human Relations Association of America came into being.

At the institute's close, there was no constitution, no clear blueprint as to what form and specific function the Association was to assume. There was no money, and little prospect of securing any appreciable amount of it this side of robbing a bank. Nevertheless, an idea was born, and that was something. Temporary officers were chosen; later, from among themselves they designated Andrew Schulze as president; Walter M. Heyne, vice-president; John C. Ballard, secretary; Martin E. Nees, treasurer; Gertrude Fiehler, membership secretary; and M. S. Dickinson, G. Hans Liebenow, and Paul Simon, directors. By November three meetings had been held, a constitution prepared, and first steps taken toward the publication of the Association's periodical to be given the title *The VANGUARD* (sub-title: The church in human relations). Professor Victor Hoffmann of Valparaiso University was appointed editor.

At the November meeting of the board of directors it was announced that the following persons had accepted appointment to the Association's advisory board: Marmaduke N. Carter, Thomas Coates, Leslie F. Frerking, Paul Friedrich, Alfred P. Klausler, O. P. Kretzmann, Theo. Kuehnert, Arthur Carl Piepkorn, Alfred M. Rehwinkel, Clemonce Sabourin, Ruben E. Spannaus, Paul W. Streufert, Otto H. Theiss, and Henry F. Wind. In 1956, E. Buckley Glabe and Louis P. Lochner, and later other persons, were added to the advisory board.

At the same meeting, Professor Paul Seehausen, who had previously been appointed by Dr. Kretzmann to serve as liaison between the University and LHRAA, reported that Dr. Kretzmann hoped LHRAA would engage an executive secretary and that he stood ready to appoint the same person to the teaching staff at Valparaiso. A committee reported, "We could begin with a modest program on a half-time basis. The executive secretary could be employed half-time by Valparaiso University if the man chosen is acceptable." After reviewing the qualifications of a

123

number of persons, the committee concluded, "We hope if and when this position is created that Andrew Schulze can fill it."

In the spring of 1954, after an agreement had been reached with Dr. Kretzmann, I was asked to become the executive secretary of LHRAA and to devote half of my time to teaching in the Theology Department. I accepted the appointment and was commissioned at the occasion of the 1954 institute.

Accepting this job was like starting on a new career, or, rather, two careers at the same time. And yet my new work was not altogether new. I was to teach theology; and although I had had a theological training of sorts and had taught religion on the parish level for 30 years, I was now to teach on the college level. That was different.

Throughout my professional life I had devoted more time to an understanding of the race problem and how to resolve it than perhaps any other clergyman of The Lutheran Church-Missouri Synod. I had been a parish pastor, and what I did in the field of race relations, though it was related to my parish ministry—and had developed out of it—was nevertheless an avocation; at least it was not my prime responsibility. It was now to become my job, my profession.

Shortly after I became a member of the faculty, Mrs. Margaretta Tangerman, then head of the Department of Sociology and Social Work, suggested that I teach a course in race relations. When such a course had been outlined and was submitted to the University's Curriculum Committee, the question arose as to whether the course should be taught in the Sociology Department or the Department of Theology. After the question had been batted back and forth for some time, the President took the matter in hand. He decided it should be offered in sociology. (At that time the university's Theology Department was under considerable fire emanating from a more conservative element in the Synod, and since the race issue was a controversial one, it is probable that Dr. Kretzmann did not want to add fuel to the fire by offering a course in race relations in that already besieged department.) Not long thereafter, though, the course was transferred to theology. I was glad for the change because the title of the course was "The Church and the Race Issue," and my main concern was the church.

My association with the Theology Department was for me both wholesome and helpful. The majority of the men in the department were young, and excited about their work. They realized that the department was in a strategic place within the framework of many academic disciplines because Valparaiso University somehow found its reason for being in the fact that it was Christian, and specifically Lutheran.

Soon after I joined the faculty, Professor Robert W. Bertram accepted the headship of the department. Together with other young colleagues he developed a curriculum that was astonishingly Scriptural and excitingly pragmatic. Although Dr. Bertram's basic discipline was theology, he had earned a master's degree in social work after his graduation from the seminary; and he put the latter into the service of the former in structuring a curriculum which attracted the attention and admiration of the heads of theology departments in other schools.

As I taught new courses that were prepared under the leadership of Dr. Bertram, I began to structure a more in-depth personal theology that affected for the better, I hope, not only the course I was already teaching, but all my work in the field of race relations as well.

LHRAA, Structure and Function

When the Lutheran Human Relations Association of America was first organized, its constituency was the St. Louis Lutheran Society for Better Race Relations, the Chicago Lutheran Society for Better Race Relations, and perhaps a hundred persons throughout the church. The Association's membership in the main was those individuals who with some degree of regularity attended the annual race relations institutes. It was assumed, though, that there were many more individual persons in many parts of the church and nation who had learned to apply the gospel of Christ to the race issue and would welcome working with the Association toward its common objective. That the Association existed, and what its purpose was, had to be made known to those already-concerned people.

In 1954 the channels of communication within the church were not open to LHRAA in keeping with the urgency of its message and program. Officials of the church body as well as parish pastors in general were not ready to "talk race" frankly, nor to work toward changing the status quo in race relations in keeping with the sweeping changes that needed to be made.

By 1970 conditions had changed. Race was still a controversial question, but it could no longer with grace and ease be swept under the rug. Nevertheless at this late hour, there was still "much land to be possessed." Many pastors, both young and old, were still unwilling or unready to help their people to become involved and to assist in wiping out racism wherever it was to be found.

In 1969 Dr. J. A. O. Preus was elected president of The Lutheran Church-Missouri Synod. Among those pastors who still believed that it was outside the realm of the church's responsibility to work directly for

125

a change in race relations, there were no doubt many who had helped to get Dr. Preus elected. Notwithstanding, on February 11, 1970, he felt compelled to write all the clergy of the Synod as follows:

The "Keys for Christ" program in our synod has not been an unmitigated success to date. I want to share with you portions of a straight-from-the-shoulder letter received from the president of Bunn Winter Associates, Inc., which had been engaged to survey the results of the campaign to date:

> Here are the tabulated results of the survey card mailing which was mailed . . . to pastors throughout the U.S.A., regarding the status of their "Keys for Christ" effort, and asking for a confirmation of their congregation's dollar contribution.
>
> *In all candidness I must say that as a Lutheran layman I am utterly disappointed with the comments and attitudes of these ordained men of God. This survey has revealed that our church's leaders are in many cases bigoted, prejudiced, and lacking in concern for their fellowman regardless of the color of his skin.* (Emphasis added)
>
> These are harsh words, Dr. Preus, but survey results like these call for something other than routine handling and judgments.
>
> Where is the compassion found in our Lord's admonition: "Inasmuch as ye have done it unto one of the least of these My brethren . . ." This survey says pointedly: It is seriously lacking in the majority of the leadership of The Lutheran Church-Missouri Synod churches.

Your first reaction, brother, may be one of anger. But let's remember that housing is one of our nation's most critical social problems. To be sure, government must be expected to take the lead in overcoming the current shortage of more than six million homes. But we in the church can make a major contribution by our involvement.

A certain definite routine developed shortly after I, in 1954, began working as the executive secretary of LHRAA and as a member of the Valparaiso faculty. This routine was followed as long as I worked in this two-fold capacity. Since I taught classes on Tuesday and Thursday, the middle of the week was devoted largely to my work for the University. The rest of the week, Friday through Monday, was in the main devoted to LHRAA responsibilities. Often I would leave Valparaiso on Thursday immediately after my last class session to travel to some metropolis like Washington, D.C., San Francisco, or New Orleans, only to return to Valparaiso on Tuesday morning in time to take up my classwork again.

Resulting primarily from the publicity we were able to get for and through the annual human relations institutes, a small number of friends among the clergy and laity understood what we were trying to do and identified themselves with us. They were our contact persons. It was chiefly through them that we were able to develop our Association and its program.

Coming to a given community, we would try to meet with those known to be favorable to what we hoped to do for the church.Whenever possible, though, arrangements were made through our cooperating friends to invite the church-public and specifically Lutherans to some church or church hall for a presentation and discussion of the race issue. A hoped-for result of these meetings was the organization of chapters of LHRAA.

During my incumbency in office about twenty such chapters came into being. They were scattered throughout the length and breadth of the nation: St. Louis, Chicago, Milwaukee, the Twin Cities, Detroit, Cleveland, Indianapolis, Cincinnati, Columbus (Ohio), Pittsburgh, Washington, D.C., Baltimore, Philadelphia, New York City, Boston, the San Francisco Bay area, Seattle, Portland (Oregon), Los Angeles, Charlotte, (N.C.), Birmingham, Tulsa, et al. Some of the chapters were short-lived; some existed for a longer period of time but with questionable virility and effectiveness. Some, however, were strong, stable, and effective.

The function of each active chapter varied. Some were education-oriented. Others combined education and action. As far as the office of LHRAA was concerned, the chapters were altogether free-wheeling; the Association did not direct the chapter program in any specific way. Their functioning was dependent upon leadership and the needs of the local community as well as the problems and opportunities peculiar to their own state.

The VANGUARD, the official organ of LHRAA, kept before its chapters and members, as well as all its readers, the purpose of the Association. It tried to alert its readers to specific race relations issues confronting the nation and the church, especially the Lutheran Church. The VANGUARD kept its readers informed on the decisions of the LHRAA board of directors, the activities of the LHRAA office and what its executive was doing under the direction of the board.

The Association was an independent organization and not an official arm of the church. The VANGUARD, as mouthpiece of the Association, was in a unique position to evaluate the status quo, to criticize when necessary, and to point to the change needed in harmony with a dynamic application of the social implications of the gospel.

In keeping with the name of its publication, the purpose of LHRAA was to help bring the church into the vanguard in the war against racism. The Association's function had a two-fold thrust: helping the church to eliminate racial discrimination in the body politic as well as in the church itself.

Every opportunity we had to further our work was seized upon: addressing pastoral conferences, young people's rallies, district conventions of the Synod, student body assemblies—especially on the campuses of preparatory schools, teachers colleges, and theological seminaries.

Soon after its organization, the Association began to direct overtures to the conventions of The Lutheran Church-Missouri Synod. These overtures were drawn up in the LHRAA office and normally submitted to pastors of congregations who were friends of the Association. They would offer the overtures to their congregations who in turn would submit them to the Synod for adoption.

The first of these overtures was addressed to the Synod at its 1956 convention in St. Paul, Minnesota. The manner in which these overtures were received and what resulted from this endeavor was discussed in a previous chapter. Following the precedent established in 1956, LHRAA directly or through other channels, memorialized the Missouri Synod at the occasion of every convention from San Francisco in 1959 to Milwaukee in 1971.

Under the guiding hand and influence of Dr. O. P. Kretzmann, Valparaiso University has supplied the Lutheran Human Relations Association of America, since the time of its organization, with a home base, with offices, office furniture, utilities, janitorial service, and less tangible goods.

In 1959, the Rev. Karl E. Lutze was added to the staff of LHRAA. At first he worked as field secretary. Later he succeeded me as executive secretary. Because of temperament, background, and dedication, he proved to be the right person to take advantage of the opportunity confronting LHRAA in the 1960's when the race issue had become so crucial as to threaten the very existence of both church and state.

Pastor Lutze also worked in a two-fold capacity, as member of the LHRAA staff and as a member of the Theology Department of the University.

Because of the intimate relationship which we enjoyed with the University, we had very close association with members of the faculty, who understood what LHRAA was trying to do and were always eager to help. If we needed legal advice, members of the School of Law came to our aid. When we needed help from other academic disciplines, history, government, biology, English, business, sociology, et al, there were always friends on the faculty ready to give assistance. And sometimes members of the University administration and faculty served our Association as members of our board of directors.

In addition to structuring the annual Valparaiso University Institutes on Human Relations, we were sometimes able, by our own suggestion, or when asked to do so, to bring outstanding speakers and programs to the campus. To mention a few such persons: the Rev. R. Ambrose Reeves, former Anglican bishop of Johannesburg, South Africa, and author of *Shooting at Sharpeville*; Judge James B. Parsons, Judge of the U.S. District Court of Northern Illinois; Dennis Brutus, of London, England, South African exile and Director of the World Campaign for the Release of South African Political Prisoners; Professor James W. Silver, author of *Mississippi: the Closed Society*.

A program which LHRAA helped to bring to the campus was "Black Nativity," written by Langston Hughes, Negro poet and playwright. It attracted much interest on the campus and in Valparaiso, and brought both praise and condemnation from many parts of the nation.

There was a similar though more intense reaction to my involvement in the Albany Movement.

In Jail in Georgia

In the preceding chapter reference was made to my participation, together with other religious leaders, in a trip to Albany, Georgia, to identify myself with the black people of that community in their common plight. The following lines are intended to show how Dr. Kretzmann and with him Valparaiso University became involved. I intend to show also the repercussions to that involvement.

Over a period of approximately ten months, black citizens representing 42 percent of the population of Albany, had tried to exercise their right as citizens "to assemble peaceably for their common good and to apply to those vested with the powers of government for redress of grievance by petition and remonstrance" (Constitution of the State of Georgia). During this period of time a total of about 1100 black people had assembled, always in small groups, in front of the city hall. In each case, instead of listening to their requests, the city authorities had them jailed.

Dr. G. W. Anderson, an osteopathic physician, was the leader of this

"Albany Movement" which involved black citizens of varied cultural and economic background. With an important gubernatorial election in the offing, and to bolster the morale of the concerned black people, Dr. Martin Luther King was asked to come to Albany. He in turn advised that religious leaders from the North be invited to come there to identify themselves with the black people in their plight.

Having received the invitation to come to Albany, and after consulting my colleague Karl Lutze, and Dr. Clemonce Sabourin, the president of LHRAA, I called Dr. Kretzmann. He gave his blessing to my going and assured me of his support. With these intangibles in hand, I sauntered forth, joining about forty more persons in Chicago, with whom I made the not too comfortable bus trip to Albany in the heart of the Southland's black belt. We were on the way thirty hours, stopping only to buy food and gasoline. It was midnight, August 27 (1962), when we arrived. The next day we made our way, 75 in all, to the city hall.

Chief of Police Laurie Pritchett with a cordon of officers was there to "welcome" us. It wasn't long before he ordered us to disperse. After repeating his mandate a second time, and when none of us moved, he gave the order to his henchmen to arrest us. After we had become the jail guests of Albany and several surrounding counties, we were kept incommunicado for two days.

When I called the president of Valparaiso, I learned that he had already received word of my incarceration, and with the help of my colleague Karl Lutze, the president had wired President Kennedy and his brother Robert, the Attorney General, as well as Chairman John A. Hannah of the U.S. Civil Rights Commission. Dr. Kretzmann then told me he would dispatch $200 bail money to secure my release.

When I had just about become conditioned to my new life in jail with its smells, bed bugs, and cockroaches all over the place, and having made the acquaintance of other humans who periodically visited the sanctuary where I was kept secluded for six days, I was released with others on Labor Day, September 3.

The telegrams and other communications emanating from the office of Dr. Kretzmann caused my involvement in the Albany visit to become known throughout the state of Indiana and in many places in The Lutheran Church-Missouri Synod. Reactions both pro and con were immediate. Most of them, but especially those protesting what I had done with the blessing of the president of the University, were directed to him and not to me. Many of these letters were forwarded to me by Dr. Kretzmann, with a humorous note written usually in the northeast corner, such as "Andy, you tell 'em," or "Andy, can you help to bring this fellow into the 20th century? O.P.K."

130

Letters of this kind were answered by me with as much dignity as I could muster befitting a letter written for a university president; and in each case a copy was sent to him. One letter came from a member of the board of directors of the University. My trip to Albany disturbed him. Among other things, he wrote, "If he is held to serve time beyond his scheduled appearance on the campus of Valparaiso University, I personally would favor withholding remuneration for the time of his absence in view of his absence apparently being due to an illegal act on his part."

When sending this letter to me, Dr. Kretzmann asked me how I would reply to it. In response, I addressed a letter to him in which I tried to cover the basic theology involved and to answer the specific criticisms raised, suggesting that he would be free to use or disregard it or any part of it, in keeping with his own discretion. Since the letter was descriptive of the problem that caused me to go to Albany as I saw it at the time, I am quoting a number of excerpts:

"The new life that we have in Christ is to be expressed in our concern for people in their suffering. By identifying ourselves with them in their need—in this instance, the removal of racial prejudice and discrimination —we follow the Scriptural directive, 'Let us not love in word and speech but in deed and truth.' By identifying ourselves with the still enslaved Negroes of the South in whatever manner time and circumstance may dictate, we are in a very meaningful manner identifying ourselves with non-white people throughout the nation as they suffer under the cruel hand of those people who use skin color as a justification for whatever type of discrimination their selfish desires may dictate.

"Now as to the suggestion made by your correspondent that my participation in the journey to Albany, Ga., made of me a violator of the law—I am convinced that there are other people within our church who would in all sincerity pass similar judgment on what I did; and I respect their opinion and concern. There are several comments that I would like to make in response to their criticism.

"The Constitution of the United States is the supreme law of the land and the Supreme Court of the United States is the 'final arbiter' of the Constitution. The Supreme Court has repeatedly interpreted the Constitution in favor of those who are working through non-violent means to rid our nation of racial discrimination. To those who would question the legality of our involvement in the Albany Movement, the First Amendment to the Constitution no doubt has something to say: 'Congress shall make no law . . . abridging the freedom of speech, or of the press; or of the right of people peaceably to assemble, and to petition the Government for redress of grievances.' And the Fourteenth Amendment to the Constitution has made the First Amendment applicable to the lib-

131

erties of persons within the confines of individual states. What is more, the action of the police of Albany in arresting people for seeking the eradication of discrimination that weighs heavily on the lives of the Negro citizens of Albany is condemned by the Constitution of the State of Georgia which says: 'The people have the right to assemble peaceably for their common good and to apply to those vested with powers of government for redress of grievances by petition or remonstrance.' "

How O.P. Felt About It

During the many years that we were privileged to work with the University, in the annual human relations institutes conducted on the campus and more specifically through the Lutheran Human Relations Association of America, we would from time to time—perhaps with a bit of apple-polishing—express our appreciation to Dr. Kretzmann for the help received from the University through him. His response was usually something to this effect, "LHRAA has done more for the University than the University has done for LHRAA." Maybe he was trying to say something similar to what Jane Addams said when asked what Sheridan Road —the wealthy people of Chicago—had done for Hull House. Her response was, "I do not know what Sheridan Road has done for Hull House; I do know what Hull House has done for Sheridan Road."

It is understandable that colleges and universities all over the land worth their salt were desirous of becoming involved in the racial revolution taking place in the early sixties. Nevertheless, because of the anticipated repercussions of such involvement coming from boards of directors, alumni, townspeople, et. al., these institutions were reluctant to go beyond a mere verbalization.

A meeting of presidents of all Indiana universities and colleges was held shortly after the Albany incident took place. Having learned how President Kretzmann and Valparaiso University had become involved, many of those attending the meeting congratulated him, so he told us as we expressed our thanks for his support at the time of the Albany jail incident.

There was no other person in a position of high administrative authority in the Lutheran Church, at least in the Missouri Synod, who understood the seriousness of the race issue and was willing, if necessary, to put his career into jeopardy by an almost unprecedented commitment to a change for the better than O. P. Kretzmann.

What has been written about Dr. Kretzmann and Valparaiso University is intended in the first place to try to help set the historical record straight. Secondly, but nevertheless with due emphasis, the above lines are intended as a personal tribute to a friend with whom I have been privileged to work directly or indirectly for almost thirty years.

There were of course many more such friends, as the next chapter indicates.

Chapter Ten

Friends and Mentors

"Männlein, Männlein, du gehst einen harten Gang," words purportedly spoken to Dr. Martin Luther, were appropriate. They are supposed to have been addressed to him by a Captain George Frundsberg as Luther was about to enter the hall in Worms to stand trial before the Roman Emperor flanked by high officials representing the Pope. All the powers of church and state were to be directed against Luther as he stood trial. Like Christ before Pontius Pilate, Luther stood alone. He was indeed, as the captain said, "walking a dangerous path."

In 1945, when I was in the center of the racial struggle as it was beginning to emerge in The Lutheran Church-Missouri Synod, the Rev. Louis Nuechterlein, then of St. Joseph, Michigan, wrote me a friendly note in obvious approval of the stand I was taking. He used the above quotation, applying it to me. But there were at that time already many friends with whom I was privileged to work and who were working with me.

Dinner Guests

The years of my professional life were spent in four cities: four years in Springfield, Illinois, nineteen in St. Louis, Missouri, seven in Chicago, and since 1954 in Valparaiso, Indiana. In all four places I had the unique privilege of coming into contact, and in many cases into close friendly association, with Lutheran students.

Springfield is a seminary town. There were always some seminarians who attended the big Trinity Church in the morning, and Holy Trinity, of which I was pastor, in the evening; some of these students assisted in Sunday school and Bible classes; many of them—and the personnel changed at least to some degree each school year—were very often guests in our little four-room parsonage at 117 North 15th Street, next door to the church.

When we moved to St. Louis, another theological seminary town, we had similar contacts with seminarians. The operation at St. Philip's in St. Louis, though, was on a much larger scale, involving many more students. In addition to their assisting in Sunday school and Bible classes as well as in a lesser degree in the three Sunday services, two morning and one evening, they helped in the Saturday School and in our work in the large segregated Homer G. Phillips Hospital across the street from the church. During the nineteen years of my pastorate at St. Philip's, probably thirty evangelistic canvasses were carried out in the immediate area of the church; the seminarians, assisted to some small degree by members of St. Philip's, were the canvassers. Another much cherished contact with seminary students during those years was at the seminary itself, where I had opportunity to lecture on race relations once or twice a year.

In 1947 we moved to Chicago where I was to begin work as a missionary-at-large on Chicago's fast-expanding southside Negro ghetto. Here too we had the opportunity of working with consecrated Lutheran students, this time from Concordia Teachers College at River Forest. For the first time in our married days there were female students taking part in the life and work of the church. This was doubly appreciated by Margaret, since our marriage was blessed with three sons, no daughters.

The work in Chicago, different from that of Springfield and St. Louis, was tough work, especially at the first church to be established under my pastorate, the Church of Christ thé King. Our contact with the River Forest students meant much to us. Their friendship and help during our seven-year residence in the Windy City were a source of encouragement and hope.

The students in Springfield, St. Louis, and Chicago were preparing for full-time work in the church, while a comparatively small number of students at Valparaiso had chosen professional church work as a career. After moving to Valparaiso in 1954, my work with university students was nevertheless in more than one way similar to that of my three previous charges. At the University I was privileged to teach students who for the most part were preparing for vocations outside the church as an institution, but who at the same time hopefully would become active church members. Here I had the unique opportunity to lecture on the social implications of the gospel, and because of many years of previous experience I was able to make specific application to the race issue.

The students who worked with me in Springfield, St. Louis, and Chicago were often dinner guests in our home on Sunday and occasionally on week-days. During those thirty years, the number of students that we—I should say, Margaret—had as guests for meals was probably more than a thousand. As I now look back, I wonder how she managed. During the earlier years there were three sons to get ready for Sunday school and church; and in a parsonage, to get them there on time was important, to set a good example for the flock, for the pastor's prestige, and all that. But about ten years of that time were depression years; and the students perhaps hoped for a menu somewhat different from what was served at the seminary or college. I recall one seminarian who, as he passed up the potatoes and waited for the meat to come his way, said, "We get plenty of potatoes at the seminary."

I hope it was without too much "malice aforethought," either toward Margaret or the students, that I welcomed having these dinner guests. Many of them, especially in the earlier years of my ministry, came to the seminary with little knowledge of what the race issue was all about. The dinner and after-dinner conversations afforded a golden opportunity to discuss the subject in an effort to prepare them for effective work at my own church and to help get them ready for the places of leadership they were soon to hold in the church.

From about 1935, and increasingly so until several years before my retirement in 1968, my lecture and preaching engagements took me to every part of the country. In many cases I was invited to lecture or preach by some of the same persons who as students had worked with me in my parish ministry or who in later years were my students. In many more cases, students, now having become clergymen or parochial school teachers, and—from among my Valparaiso students—professional people, were not only present when I lectured or preached, but were also active in their churches and communities, promoting race relations in keeping with good Christian ethics.

Friends When the Going was Tough

The depression years during the thirties were tough years in more than one sense. "Last to be hired and first to be fired" was more than a cliche; it was a stark reality that affected every Negro community in the United States. St. Louis, Missouri, and St. Philip's congregation in that city were no exception. Very often the congregation was three to four months in arrears in the payment of my salary. And this was merely a reflection of a deeper problem when perhaps 25 to 50 percent of the employable members of the congregation were either unemployed altogether or trying to make ends meet on the checks doled out by the Federal Government on such projects as Emergency Relief, WPA, and CCC.

During those depression years, friends who could give material help were hard to find. There was an organization of dedicated Lutheran women in St. Louis, at that time called the Ladies Aid for Negro Missions. They were always ready to help in keeping with their own financial limitations.

I recall that when I was about ten years old, my parochial school teacher had lectured on the development of will power. Thirsty as I was on returning home from a hotly contested ball game on an equally hot day, I rushed to the cistern pump behind our house and was about to drink a tin-cupful of cold water that I had pumped for myself, when I remembered my teacher's lesson. Instead of drinking the water, I poured it on the lawn. How often thereafter I disciplined myself in the same manner, I do not remember. But the proverbial "cup of cold water" extended by a friend in a time of great loneliness can be an exhilarating experience to be remembered long after the loneliness has disappeared.

In the dry and thirsty land of the thirties and early forties, my loneliness was seldom if ever spelled out. Those who at that time were speaking against racism in the world and ignorance and indifference in the church toward racism were indeed following a lonely path, and "a cup of cold water" offered by some friend who understood was like the "balm in Gilead." Such was my experience when the Rev. Martin C. Schaefer, at that time pastor of St. Paul Church in St. Louis, would phone, inviting me to be defeated once again in a game of handball. At times he suggested that our families should have a picnic in an East St. Louis park. More importantly, in the early winter of 1942 he told the St. Louis Pastoral Conference that he had read in one sitting my book, *My Neighbor of Another Color*, which had just been published and which he challenged our ministerial colleagues to study. Many St. Louis pastors of that time were trying to evade the issue and, I suppose, trying to stay out of my way.

It was Dr. Alfred M. Rehwinkel who defended the essay I read before a pastoral conference in 1938, as he stretched out his long arms and said, "This opens up a vast vista of opportunity for the church." For many years thereafter, when the going was hard for those who were desirous of helping the church to rid itself of indifference and sloth in matters racial, Dr. Rehwinkel proved to be a strong and articulate friend. When the first draft of *My Neighbor of Another Color* was finished, he invited me to visit him in his home where I read aloud from one copy of the manuscript while he followed from another and made helpful comments and criticisms. In keeping with the dauntless character of the man, and with possible anticipation of bitter opposition on the part of some of his colleagues on the St. Louis seminary faculty, he wrote a foreword to the book.

Dr. Rehwinkel became the first president of the St. Louis Lutheran

Society for Better Race Relations. He was a member of the editorial staff of the *Lutheran Race Relations Bulletin*. For many years he lectured and preached on the church and the race issue. In later years he became a member of the Advisory Board of the Lutheran Human Relations Association of America. Although, ironically, in the 1960's he seemingly became an advocate of racial segregation, I shall not forget his friendship, and hope to remain grateful to God and him for the assistance he gave in earlier years.

G. Hans Liebenow, often referred to in these pages, was a student at the St. Louis seminary when my book came on the market. He became my unsolicited, unpaid colporteur, trying to sell the book to professors, students, and synodical officials, including Dr. Behnken, the Texas-reared president of The Lutheran Church-Missouri Synod.

Dr. Walter A. Maier, originator of the Lutheran Hour and its first speaker, was a man of great evangelistic fervor. When he learned that my church, St. Philip's, was figuratively bursting at its seams and that we hoped to divert many of our mission prospects—some of whom had become interested in the Lutheran Church through the Lutheran Hour— to another area about a mile distant from my church, he wanted to help. He became the chairman of an ad hoc committee that had as its goal the raising of funds for the erection of a chapel at the new location. When the cornerstone of the chapel was laid, the new mission church was named Holy Sacraments Lutheran Church. Dr. Maier was the preacher for this festive occasion. Although he was a great friend of missions and had devoted much of his precious time to this specific project, his passion for the eternal salvation of people caused him at least on occasion to overlook the unity effected by the Holy Spirit, to be evidenced in the togetherness of them that believe. For example, in his cornerstone-laying address he pictured, to my dismay and that of others, the development of "a whole chain of *Negro* Lutheran churches" and a Negro Lutheran seminary in St. Louis.

As a result of the Lutheran Hour, a number of Negroes in Pittsburgh wrote to the Lutheran Hour expressing interest in the Lutheran Church. The outcome was the beginning of a mission in a Negro community of that city. Soon thereafter Dr. Maier in a Lutheran Hour sermon referred to the establishment of the new mission, and with his usual fervor exhorted Christians everywhere to establish *Negro* missions or churches. I wrote him, calling his attention to the fact that many would interpret his remarks as advocating segregation in the church. I suggested also that he would do well in the future to exhort churches in their missionary outreach to include the Negroes of their communities. He replied promptly to my letter by saying the objectionable wording of the sermon was being changed before the sermon would be printed and sent to listeners requesting it; and in the future he would follow my suggestion when referring to winning Negroes for the church. The humility of this great man of God should be remembered above the mistakes he made.

When I left St. Louis, the mantle of loneliness fell on the shoulders of my successor, the Rev. Walter M. Heyne. By 1949 when Pastor Heyne became pastor of St. Philip's, Negroes were moving into the communities of many St. Louis Lutheran churches and many of the financial pillars of the churches were moving into the suburbs and transferring their membership to suburban congregations. St. Philip's, though, was prospering in terms of dollars and numbers.

Some of the leaders among the clergy of St. Louis at first told Pastor Heyne, "You are different from Schulze. We can listen to you." When they found out, however, that, basically, he had the same approach to the race issue as I, his counsel too was avoided. The St. Louis Pastoral Conference, by force of circumstances, had now been compelled to face the issue of race. Pastor Heyne had many years' experience as the pastor of white congregations, but he was now the pastor of a predominantly Negro congregation of potential influence. As a result of his experience in both fields, he could well have given the conference helpful counsel. Nevertheless, he too was largely ignored; and in his loneliness had to look elsewhere for clergy rapport, companionship, and inspiration.

Since social thought to a great extent is conditioned by social environment, it is not surprising that Christian social workers and social scientists in the thirties and forties were among the leaders in the church who both understood the church's backwardness in the area of race relations and were working in their sphere of influence for a God-intended and God-pleasing change. Among many more, the names of Dr. Henry F. Wind and Dr. E. Buckley Glabe are worthy of special mention. It is altogether understandable that they were selected to become members of the Advisory Board of LHRAA after it was organized.

Another social scientist of some renown in his day was E. G. Steger. A graduate of Concordia Seminary in St. Louis, he later became executive director of the Social Planning Council of St. Louis and St. Louis County. Somewhat like Melchizedek of old, he appeared on the scene but once and at that time made a deep impression on me which was to influence my thinking and activity from then on.

I met Mr. Steger at the Walther League Camp Arcadia. As we sat on the shore of Lake Michigan one summer day in 1935, I found in him—as I had found in few before that time—a man who understood the social implications of the gospel, the profound lag in our American culture specifically in the area of race, and the disrepute into which the church had fallen because of its inability or unwillingness to use its dynamic power in the interest of racial justice. Suffice it to say at this point, he counseled that Lutherans in the St. Louis area be called together to form an association that would address itself to this need. After that casual meeting on the shore of Lake Michigan, and resulting from his advice, the St. Louis Lutheran Society for Better Race Relations, described in the previous chapter, was organized.

Mention has already been made of the support given by Dr. O. H. Theiss through a review he wrote of *My Neighbor of Another Color*, published in *The Cresset*. His friendship was constant during the hectic forties. On many occasions his counsel and help were sought and freely given. Professor Theiss was chosen to be a member of the Advisory Board of the Lutheran Human Relations Association of America. By awarding him, posthumously, the Association's Mind of Christ Award in 1962, LHRAA also recognized the staunch support he had given.

While Dr. Theiss was executive secretary of the International Walther League, Dr. Thomas Coates was a member of the League's executive staff. He, like Dr. Theiss, proved to be a staunch and able friend. This became even more evident when he became president of Concordia College in Portland, Oregon, and later when he was chairman of the Religion Department of Concordia Senior College in Fort Wayne, Indiana. For many years he was a member of the Board of Directors of LHRAA, in which capacity he rendered distinguished service.

Miss Anne M. Engelbrecht must be numbered among the many friends who could be trusted to help in time of need. For many years, and until her retirement in the early sixties, she was office manager for Scott, Foresman & Company in Chicago. Anne was a leading spirit in the organization and development of the 1948 and 1949 Lutheran Human Relations Institutes in Chicago. She had a big hand in the organization in 1948 of the Chicago Lutheran Society for Better Race Relations. After supporting the Valparaiso University Institutes on Human Relations from 1950 to 1953, helping toward the organization of LHRAA, she was elected to membership on its board of directors.

Miss Engelbrecht's deep commitment to the cause is evidenced by her transferring her membership from a suburban congregation to First Immanuel Church in Chicago when it became the first Lutheran congregation of that city to carry out an integration program. At this writing, and despite many inconveniences and perhaps some danger, her membership is still at First Immanuel.

Many of those spoken of as friends in the preceding pages of this chapter have been mentors as well; and almost all of those spoken of in the following lines as mentors were also friends. The reason for making what might be an arbitrary distinction will perhaps become apparent to the reader as we move forward.

Some of these my mentors were people of learning. But what intrigued me most was what I learned from very lowly, humble folk, some of whom never went to school in their lives—learning which shapes character, deepens convictions, and helps to set one on the road that he will travel the remainder of his earthly sojourn.

Taught by Mrs. Bates

Mrs. George Bates was a member of Holy Trinity congregation in Springfield, Illinois. I met her when, upon invitation of her husband, I came to worship at Holy Trinity the first Sunday after arriving in Springfield to study at the theological seminary in that town. I was privileged to become intimately acquainted with her. From many conversations I had with this intelligent and cultured woman when I was a student, and later her pastor, a few reminiscences. But first a few more words about her husband.

Although he attended the church services regularly and participated in many of its activities, Mr. Bates was not a member when I first became acquainted with him. And why? He was a Mason; and anyone acquainted with Missouri Synod polity at that time will remember that a Mason could not get into the kingdom of God with a ten-foot pole, at least not via the Missouri Synod. It was one of the highlights of my early parish ministry when I was privileged to welcome into the fellowship of the church through baptism and confirmation, Mr. Bates, the man who first brought me into contact with Negro Lutherans.

After I had become the pastor of Holy Trinity congregation, Mrs. Bates told me of a traumatic experience and how, as she felt, the church had deserted her in an hour of great need. Her son, a member of the congregation, who had recently married, committed suicide, but her pastor would not perform a burial ceremony, nor even hold a private service in her home.

Mrs. Bates' sister, who also was a Lutheran, died in my home town, Cincinnati. (It was general practice at that time that the body of the deceased would be brought to the church where the funeral service was conducted.) Mrs. Bates told me what a shock it was to her when the pastor of a Missouri Synod Lutheran church in Cincinnati refused to give her sister the honor of a church funeral; and the obvious reason was her racial identity.

These anecdotes illustrate not only the problems for the faithful when a more or less legalistic interpretation of the church's doctrine is strictly enforced, but also the special measure of grace needed to remain faithful when an element of racial discrimination becomes a part of such doctrinaire pastoral ministry.

Through my contact with the Bateses I learned in the early days of my parish ministry what the seminary classroom lectures could not impart —a lesson that was to stand me in good stead for many years to come.

In the early twenties, with full steam ahead, the Synodical Conference was opening Christian day schools, establishing new preaching stations, and adding an impressive number of converts from among the Negroes in the Black Belt of Alabama. Mrs. Bates asked me what at that time was an embarrassing though quite relevant question about our mission work in that state.

There were many reasons for asking the question. The Rev. George A. Schmidt, superintendent of the work in Alabama, had been her pastor in Springfield. He was a dynamic missionary, overflowing with zeal for the kingdom of God as he understood it. Mrs. Bates herself being identified racially with the people with whom we were working in Alabama was therefore by personal experience well acquainted with the total need of the people in question. In substance, she asked: When bringing the gospel to the people of the Black Belt, what was our church doing about the inhuman injustices that were weighing down on them?

I remember quite well the nature of my answer. It was couched in terms of the theology I had imbibed, and was a defense of that theology and the practice ensuing from it: the church, while silently deploring these injustices, was working within the structure of that Southern society and, without a confrontation with it, was "preaching the gospel, to save souls."

I knew full well that my answer was not satisfactory, not for her and surely not for me. The question as well as my answer haunted me for twenty years or more, until my theology, at least in this respect, had changed.

The question raised by Mrs. Bates, and the implied criticism of the church, prompt me to hold her name in high esteem not only as a friend, but also as a mentor.

Superintendent of Negro Orphanage

There was a small orphanage for Negro children in Springfield. In the fall of 1924, shortly after I had become the pastor of Holy Trinity, a number of children from the orphanage began attending Sunday school. I called at the orphanage to express my interest in the children.

The woman in charge was a Negro. From the conversation that ensued, I gathered that she was both educated and intelligent. She asked me why I was interested in these children. In my youthful naivete and in response to an altogether unexpected question which perhaps implied an element of criticism, I replied: "I want to help destroy the kingdom of Satan and to build up the kingdom of Jesus Christ." She responded, "Young man, you have taken on a mighty big job."

In later years I often wondered whether her understanding of the two kingdoms was different from mine, and, since my seminary theology had led me to accept a clear-cut dichotomy between body and soul, whether her concept of the kingdom of Christ and the kingdom of Satan was not closer to the truth than my own.

Some of the Lowly-Mentors to Me

The words of wisdom attributed to the late Adlai E. Stevenson when he was governor of Illinois may be appropriate here: "Many things are revealed to the humble that are hidden to the great."

When I met Mrs. Bettie Washington in 1928 as I became the pastor of St. Philip's Church in St. Louis, she was about 80 years old. She told me that as a slave girl in Virginia, in the house of her master, she had on more than one occasion served John Brown, the great abolitionist, at table. If my memory serves me correctly, she told me her master cooperated with the Underground Railroad movement which had as its purpose smuggling slaves out of the South. It was in that capacity, according to Mrs. Washington, that her master had clandestinely acted as host to John Brown.

The husband, Mr. Washington, was probably several years older than his wife. He too had been a slave. When he was 14 years old he ran away from his master who apparently was also his father.

George Washington was the sexton at St. Philip's Church; and what a sexton he was! While he was in charge, the church premises and the church were kept immaculate. (It was a weekly ritual of his to dust even the steam pipes suspended from the ceiling in the basement assembly room.) Any offense against the church and the premises was considered a personal offense against him. In this matter he was altogether impartial; the boys from the parsonage next door were reprimanded like others when their turn came.

143

Although Mr. Washington had never attended school, he had learned to read simple materials. Very often, when I passed the boiler room, I would find him—his work for the time completed—sitting there with a primary Sunday school leaflet in hand, reading. When I greeted him, he would look up and refer to the Bible story before him; and if the text suggested it, would comment on the love of "our Savior." He was to me an outstanding example of a Christian gentleman.

It is one thing to be taught in the classroom how to recognize and respect people of integrity. It is another thing to learn through personal experience that people like Mr. and Mrs. George Washington are persons of exceptional Christian character and uprightness.

Mrs. Margaret Pitts was born, so she said, "in the second year of freedom." I assume that what she meant by "freedom" was either the Emancipation Proclamation or the end of the Civil War. She too had never gone to school and, what is more, she had not learned to do much more than to keep her house clean and to wash clothes. Many a time as I sat in the study of the parsonage of St. Philip's Church I saw Mrs. Pitts passing by with a basket of laundry on her head. (You modern women with electric washers and dryers at your disposal, try it some bright Monday morning.)

When on occasion I would make a pastoral or sick call on Mrs. Pitts, it would always be a refreshing experience. She had grasped the simple truths of the freedom we have through the gospel of Christ and in her unsophisticated and unostentatious way would bear witness to her child-like faith. Though I have learned from St. Francis of Assisi to pray "not so much to be consoled as to console," I was consoled, and strengthened in my faith, through the witness of this plain, pious Christian woman.

He was "an Israelite indeed, in whom is no guile" (John 1:47).

Among the hundreds of adults whom I was privileged to confirm, there is no name that stands out more indelibly than that of William H. Lockman. He came from Mississippi, near Vicksburg, where a decent schooling for black children was hard to come by. Having moved with his wife and five children to St. Louis, he told me, "I am glad to be *from* Mississippi."

Coming into the Lutheran Church was to him an experience like finding "a pearl of great price." At the time, several of his children were married, but his sturdy Christian character influenced all of his children as well as his invalid wife to become members of the Lutheran Church. When, because of the rapid growth of his congregation (with three services each Sunday) a daughter church was being planned, Mr. Lockman accompanied me as I went among fellow Lutherans of the St. Louis area to help raise funds for the erection of a chapel to accommodate the contemplated daughter church.

Dr. Walter A. Maier of Lutheran Hour fame invited me to meet with a select group of people whom he wanted to interest in the chapel project. One person in the group was the widow of the millionaire Lutheran soap manufacturer, Louis Waltke. Mr. Lockman accompanied me to the meeting. He, a man of humble birth and very little education, addressed the group with dignity, sincerity, and eloquence. When he finished, Dr. Maier embraced him with all the fervor of spirit typical of his inimitable personality.

When in 1947 I moved to Chicago, Mr. Lockman too had moved there. As the race issue was more and more engaging the attention of the church as well as society in general, Mr. Lockman identified himself with those in the church who had committed themselves to the task of helping to improve the church's image in the area of race relations. As he attended the annual Valparaiso University Human Relations Institutes year after year, his dignified Christian character, his very presence and humble participation gave others courage to lend the weight of their influence to the cause of the institutes.

The Holy Spirit can and does use the most humble people to accomplish His purpose in the church. Mr. Lockman's formal schooling was that of a scant three years in a Mississippi school system which, for Negro children, could hardly be called a system. Several years before his death, when he was nearing his eightieth year, he told me in confidence that he had gone to night school and had just received his eighth grade certificate.

Mr. Lockman was to me not only a personal friend and a source of encouragement, but a mentor as well.

A Mother to Many

Miss Fauline Craig was a visiting public school nurse in St. Louis. Although she was not wealthy, she (possibly together with her sister Sarah) had inherited the old homestead and had built a new residence on the adjoining property. She had received what, for Negroes living in St. Louis under the pall of racial segregation and discrimination, was a good education. Having learned and accepted the freedom that is ours in Christ, she used it to serve Him by serving others, especially children. Her inheritance, her education, her professional know-how and skill were dedicated to such service.

When writing about Miss Craig, I am reminded of words attributed to a Northhamptonshire cobbler-preacher, William Carey, who later became one of the greatest missionaries in modern times to bring the Good News of Christ to India. While still plying his trade as a cobbler in England, he is supposed to have said, "My business is to preach the gospel; I cobble shoes to pay the expenses." So it was with Miss Craig; all her mental and physical resources were used in service to Christ and children.

Dr. Comissiong, a physician and surgeon living in St. Louis, decided to return to his native home, Trinidad, but didn't want to take his big new Buick with him. Knowing the service Miss Craig was rendering to many deprived children of the community, he wanted her to have the Buick, and sold it to her "for a song." She found good use for it: each Sunday morning, shortly before the beginning of Sunday school, the Buick would pull up to the Goode Avenue entrance of St. Philip's Church, and children, as many as a dozen, would pour out of the car.

During the hey-day of St. Philip's numerical growth, on several Sundays during the year the main service featured the baptism of children. Sometimes there were as many as twenty, and on one occasion there were thirty-two. And in each group there were a goodly number whom, with their parents, Miss Craig had interested in the church.

Fully conscious of the inhuman injustices heaped upon otherwise innocent black people in a racist society and in the church, Miss Craig did not allow herself to become soured toward the church and its life-giving freedom in Christ. Many who were brought to Christ through the dedicated service of Miss Craig (including a young black man, Professor George Campbell, now teaching at Alabama Lutheran Academy and College) will on the Great Day rise up to call her blessed.

Although I was often very slow in following her good example, I nevertheless learned much from Miss Craig.

"You Brought Me to Christ"

Otis E. Finley, Sr., physical education instructor and football coach at Vashon High School, and Mrs. Finley, became members of St. Philip's Church in St. Louis in 1930. They had found in the Lutheran Church that which they had been seeking for themselves and their sons.

Richard K. Fox, Sr. was at that time a mathematics instructor at Sumner, the other Negro high school in St. Louis. The Finleys and the Foxes were close friends. The Finleys began to tell the Foxes about the Lutheran Church as they had learned to know it. The Foxes were impressed. Mr. Finley invited Mr. Fox to worship with him some Sunday morning. Though Mr. Fox was reluctant at first, the Foxes came, and soon came again. They became members of the congregation, and their children as well. It wasn't long before Mr. Fox became the congregation's treasurer, later also Sunday school superintendent.

Fifteen years passed by, when in 1947 I had accepted a call that was to take my family and me to Chicago. My farewell sermon was preached on Sunday morning. In the evening there was a farewell service and "reception" at the church. Members stopped by at the parsonage from Monday to Thursday to convey a personal and final farewell. On Thursday morning the movers came. While our household belongings were being removed, and late into the afternoon, members of the congregation kept dropping in to speak a final word.

Shortly before we were to leave for the railroad station, Mr. and Mrs. Fox arrived. Mr. Fox told me that he and his wife would like to say a few words to me in private. At the moment the only place for privacy in the parsonage was in the kitchen, so I escorted the Foxes there.

Mrs. Fox, who was normally a reserved person, usually glad to have others do the talking, came up to me with what seemed to be an unusual amount of courage and said, "Pastor, I want to tell you before you leave that you brought me to Christ." And Mr. Fox added, "and that applies to me and our entire family."

What a farewell gift! What God-pleasing humility the Holy Spirit works in the hearts of men! What a glorious confession of "the name which is above every name" (Phil. 2:9). Those few words of the Foxes in the kitchen of the vacant parsonage taught me as perhaps nothing else in my entire pastoral life what St. Paul meant when he wrote, "Ye are all the children of God by faith in Christ Jesus. . . . There is neither Jew nor Greek, there is neither bond nor free, there is neither male nor female; for *ye are all one in Christ Jesus*" (Gal. 3:26, 28, KJV).

Clemonce Sabourin, Man of Courage and Determination

In 1938, the depression was still very much in evidence in the land, and my congregation—St. Philip's in St. Louis—and Grace Mission of the same city, both having an almost exclusively Negro membership, had no funds earmarked for travel expenses. The Rev. John W. C. Fey of Grace Mission, Albert T. Jefferson, a lay delegate from St. Philip's, and I pooled our financial resources to make the trip in my old Franklin "limousine" to a General Conference meeting at Immanuel College in Greensboro, N.C.

More than ten years had passed. Many committee meetings had been held and not a few reports made, but with no discernible progress: the congregations represented at the General Conference meeting were not in any manner integrated; organic union with the Synodical Conference or any of its constituent synods seemed as far away as it was in 1920 or

1927. But the race issue was now boiling beneath the surface, and the delegates to the Greensboro conference, Negro as well as Caucasian, for the most part had no sure sense of direction. The danger was present that the delegates, 75 percent of them pastors, would sweep the race issue under the rug, and Uncle Tom and Jim Crow would have another lease on life in the church.

Synodical Conference officials were not inclined to work toward a change in the status quo. Pastors and missionaries beholden to the officials for their salaries and their jobs were on the whole reluctant to address themselves vigorously to the question of racism in the church. They were not even ready to address themselves to the dual wage system which compelled many of the Negro workers to live below the subsistence level of the white workers.

While all of this was evident at the General Conference meeting for those who had eyes to see, young Pastor Sabourin, though knowing on which side his bread was buttered, spoke out against the system that tolerated, condoned, or fostered racism in the church. With the cutting sword of the unvarnished truth he lashed out against the status quo people in the audience and those who he thought had forgotten the either-or attitude of Christ who said, "he who is not with me is against me" (Matt. 12:30).

Shortly after we started on our homeward journey, the conversation centered on Pastor Sabourin. One of our travel companions volunteered the remark, "Watch that fellow Sabourin. We must foster his friendship. God can and possibly will use him in a big way to establish His purpose in the church."

It seems to me that I did not enjoy the confidence of Pastor Sabourin at the Greensboro conference. Although I had until then been more forthright than most of my colleagues in castigating the evils of racism in the church, Pastor Sabourin perhaps wanted to try me out before cultivating anything that might be described as a close personal friendship. But by the time we met again—in 1942—true friendship had been established between us.

Thirteen years after the 1938 General Conference meeting in Greensboro, one of our sons was a newlywed. He took his wife with him to the Atlantic District convention. Shortly after the close of the convention Pastor Sabourin wrote me among other things: "It was nice of your son to bring his wife out to see us while he was in New York City. But tell me, how in the world did you manage so completely to confound your enemies? Your idea of having mixed congregations is supposed to lead to mixed marriages. (Not long ago a friend of mine said something complimentary about me to a friend of his. The reply was, 'Yes, Sabourin

148

may be all right. But he is just as bad as Andrew Schulze. He advocates mixed marriages.')

"Now your son was brought up in a mixed congregation. Surely he met and associated with many Negro girls. How did he escape the peril? And you, have you lost your influence? Surely any agitator worthy of the name should be able to do a good job with his son. The point is this: If you are going to maintain your reputation as a corruptor of our youth, you will have to remember that corruption begins at home."

The relationship between Pastor Sabourin and me developed into something more than close friendship. I was privileged on more than one occasion to find him leading me away from the quicksands of gradualism where gradualism had no justification in Christian theology.

The most outstanding example of the helpful leadership of Pastor Sabourin was evidenced when he and I were members of a committee appointed by the Synodical Conference in 1944 to try to resolve the question of future affiliation or non-affiliation of General Conference congregations with the Synodical Conference and its constituent synodical members. (The work of this committee is related in some detail in the chapter on Conferences and Church Conventions.) When we worked together on this Advisory Committee, I had more background, in a sense, than he: I had been president of the General Conference for 14 years and had spent 20 years in the parish ministry, while he had been in the ministry about 10 years. He nevertheless provided the chief leadership, which caused the committee to recommend and the Synodical Conference in 1946 to adopt the committee's recommendation which opened the door for congregations of black membership to be admitted into membership of constituent synods of the Synodical Conference.

Clemonce Sabourin has been to me a mentor, as well as a friend, in that he very often showed me the way. In recognition of the leadership given to the church in the area of race relations, Valparaiso University in 1963 conferred on him the honorary degree of Doctor of Laws.

Much has been written in previous chapters showing the inadequacy of the theology of the church in the area of race relations, and, resulting from that, the less than good response on the part of many to the need for eradicating racism. But there were always some among the clergy as well as the laity who saw the light and were guided by it. This is what prompted the inclusion of a chapter on Friends and Mentors. It should be emphasized, however, that, in addition to those mentioned, there were many more with whom I was privileged to work who were a source of strength, help, and hope to me.

149

Afterword

There are a number of purposes for witnessing to Jesus Christ through the good news about Him, the final object of all of them being the praise and glory of God. Basic to this proclamation of the gospel is man's eternal salvation. If the church is to be and remain faithful to Christ, it must always remain faithful to the teaching and preaching of the good news summarized by Christ Himself in the words, "God so loved the world that he gave his only Son, that whoever believes in him should not perish but have eternal life" (John 3:16).

It is of the essence of the church's commitment to Christ to point to the reconciliation of God to man effected through the death of Jesus Christ, the once-for-all event called the vicarious atonement. It is also of the very nature of this commitment to urge the estranged man "living without Christ and without hope in the world" (Eph. 2:13) to accept God's already effected reconciliation with the full hope of a resurrection to life everlasting in heaven. The Missouri Synod probably has not been found wanting with respect to this basic element of witness. Together with other denominations, the Missouri Synod has also taught and preached that personal morality, living an honest, decent, and upright life, is a necessary fruit of faith to be nurtured at all times.

Nor has the church forgotten altogether its responsibility to urge its people to give to the needy, to care for the sick and the aged, and to participate in other similar types of Christian social welfare. However, from the perspective of our present concern—the church and the race issue—the Missouri Synod, not unlike other major denominations, was slow to comprehend and to act according to such comprehension that our Christian responsibility is not fulfilled merely by trying somehow to bind up wounds, a laudable though limited function of social welfare.

There is something basically wrong in the body politic which forms the structure in which a society condones, accepts, and perhaps thrives on flagrant injustice such as was the lot of black people in the United States under a system of chattel slavery and later of racial segregation. It is necessary for the church in its teaching and preaching, and its people in their civic life and action, to strike at the Achilles heel of the unjust political system itself. This is especially true in a constitutional democracy such as ours. Theoretically at least, we, the people, are the government; the senators and representatives in Congress, who make the laws and supply or withhold the funds needed to make the laws effective, are our representatives. They are our servants who work for us.

In the final analysis *we* are responsible for justice in the land and dare not hide behind the flimsy excuse, "That's the government's business." Through our own personal concern and action justice is to be done (Micah 6:8). Noncommittal silence must be dispensed with, dispersed by the winds of the Spirit who in that "still small voice" puts these words in our hearts and upon our lips: I am my brother's keeper (Gen. 4:9).

The gospel of eternal salvation through the death and resurrection of Jesus Christ and the social implications of the gospel are as inseparable as Siamese twins; separate them and both will die. But when the gospel and its social implications are properly kept together in teaching and practice, the Lord of heaven and earth is truly glorified in the church.

There is, however, a tendency today among some church leaders to take for granted, to ignore, or to bypass in their teaching and attitude in general the otherworldly basic element in the Christian proclamation and life. They would have the pendulum of theology and Christian witness not only to swing to the left, but to stick there. Dr. Martin H. Scharlemann in *The Church's Social Responsibilities* (St. Louis: Concordia Publishing House, 1971) warns against the danger inherent in this tendency: ". . . a totally secularized order of life is one that has no center. While it may create a certain tolerable equilibrium, this balance is extremely tenuous. The scales can quickly tip toward secularism, which is, for all practical purposes, a new religion, comprising a faith of a single dimension that tends to close our universe by destroying an awareness of and interest in what is transcendental. When this happens, life may even be reduced to the level of nihilism, whose basis is a disbelief in any and all powers and whose only product can be a spiritual desert of unending void" (pp. 59-60).

Dr. Scharlemann writes further, "When Christians undertake creative solutions, the Lutheran Church insists [yes, the church must insist] that they carry on such work with a motivation quite different from that of other men and institutions. In its case, for instance, the ministry to persons in need will not shrink to case work but will constitute a service for which God provides strength. The church's care for the needy is not mere charity, not the mere giving of gifts, for Christians know that a person must give of himself to practice love" (pp. 78-79).

When a ship with hundreds of passengers aboard is listing to one side and in danger of capsizing, the captain will not counsel the passen-

151

gers to move to the center of the deck; he will tell them to rush to the opposite side. The emphasis in this book on certain social implications of the gospel, i.e., social concern and social action, is made with the hope of helping to save the ship of the church, not only from disrepute before the world, but also from the danger of capsizing due to an overweighted otherworldly theology. An understanding of our past and the ultraconservative attitude of many in the church today, especially among the affluent, middle-class laymen, of which there are not a few, justifies in my mind the procedure I have followed.

Let both have their due—the gospel of eternal salvation focused on eternal life in heaven, and the social implications of the gospel focused on man's here-and-now needs—and the church militant will live on triumphantly until it has merged forever with the church triumphant in heaven.

Biographical Notes

Born March 8, 1896, Cincinnatio, Ohio.
Overseas duty with the U.S. Navy in World War I.
Graduated from Concordia Seminary, Springfield, Illinois, 1924.

Served as pastor of churches in Negro communities over a period of thirty years: Springfield, Illinois (1924-28); St. Louis, Missouri (1928-47); Chicago, Illinois (1947-54).

Chairman of General Conference of churches in Negro communities 1930-46.

Member of Mayor's Commission on Race Relations, St. Louis, 1944-47.
Member of Synodical Conference Mission Survey Committee, 1944-46.
Member of Missionary Board of the Synodical Conference, 1946-52.

Author of *My Neighbor of Another Color*, a treatise on race relations in the church, published in 1941; and *Fire from the Throne*, a further treatise on the church and the race issue, published in 1968. Author of many articles on race relations published in various periodicals.

Editor and chief writer of *Lutheran Race Relations Bulletin*, 1945-50. Editor of *The Vanguard*, publication of the Lutheran Human Relations Association of America, 1954-1963.

Helped to organize the annual Valparaiso University Human Relations Institutes, and Lutheran Human Relations Societies in many cities.

In June 1954 accepted a joint appointment by the Lutheran Human Relations Association of America and Valparaiso University. In this two-fold capacity, functioned as Executive Secretary of LHRAA (1954-64) and taught part-time in the Department of Theology at the University (1954-68).

Director of Research of the Lutheran Human Relations Association of America, 1964-68.

One of seventy-five religious leaders arrested in Albany, Georgia, in August 1962, when they identified themselves with the plight of the black people of that city.

By invitation of the late President John F. Kennedy, participated in the White House Conference of Religious Leaders June 17, 1963.

LL.D. degree (honoris causa) conferred by Valparaiso University, 1953. Recipient of the Mind of Christ Award, 1963. Doctor of Divinity degree (honoris causa) conferred by Concordia Theological Seminary, St. Louis, 1966.